SPEAKING OF INDIA

Bridging the Communication Gap When Working with Indians

Craig Storti

INTERCULTURAL PRESS
A Nicholas Brealey Publishing Company

BOSTON • LONDON

First published by Intercultural Press, a division of Nicholas Brealey Publishing, in 2007.

Intercultural Press,
a division of Nicholas Brealey Publishing
20 Park Plaza, Suite 1115A
Boston, MA 02116, USA
Tel: + 617-523-3801
Fax: + 617-523-3708
www.interculturalpress.com

Nicholas Brealey Publishing
3-5 Spafield Street, Clerkenwell
London, EC1R 4QB, UK
Tel: +44-(0)-207-239-0360
Fax: +44-(0)-207-239-0370
www.nicholasbrealey.com

Printed in the United States of America

13 12 11 10 09   2 3 4 5 6

ISBN-13: 978-1-931930-34-5
ISBN-10: 1-931930-34-1

Library of Congress Cataloging-in-Publication Data

Storti, Craig.
   Speaking of India : bridging the communication gap when working with Indians / Craig Storti.
        p. cm.
   Includes bibliographical references.
   ISBN 1-931930-13-9
   1. .Communication and culture—India.   2. Communication—Cross-cultural studies.   3. Interpersonal communication—Cross-cultural studies.   I. Title.
   P94. 65.I4S76 2007
   303.48'25401821—dc22

                                                                2007030434

To Marty McCaffrey,
who made all this possible

Contents

Foreword

Often in business, culture is undervalued. While cash rules, the impact of culture is more subtle, less measurable, and consequently does not stay on the leadership radar. In the transnational context, this is far more marked as cultural facets are less understood and more powerful. In almost mysterious fashion, deals come undone, initiatives get gridlocked, relationships founder, and mergers or acquisitions fall way short of promise. When things go wrong, the visible sides of the cultural coin are ignorance and arrogance. This is a pity. Even at a personal level, insularity denies us the awesome quality of a rich world experience, be it language, art, religion, tradition, custom, music, cuisine, architecture, or simply the attire and the accent.

Craig Storti's book is both timely and insightful. India as an economy and as a market is once again relevant. The opportunism of the traders and the insidious dominance of the colonialists have given way to the spirit of collaborative enterprise. But the mindsets around the table carry the imagery of the past. This needs unlearning and refreshing. This book is a great start on the journey of cultural appreciation. Usefully, it grounds the understanding in the context of business transactions. By using the mode of day-to-day conversations, a complex subject is made accessible. Herein lies the brilliance of *Speaking of India*.

The Do Re Mi of Western classical music is similar to the Sa Re Ga of Indian classical music. Yet, the music is played differently—one from a sheet, another from memory. Listeners, too, absorb the compositions very differently. Each genre of music is, in a sense, a reflection of the underlying culture. A symphony is structured for consistency, while a raaga comes alive differently with each rendition. But the fusion of these two very similar, yet very different, forms has resulted in an art form born of experimentation and understanding by artists from both genres.

Likewise, in the metaphor of business, Storti's book gives us an appreciation of how we can find the common ground. Standing together on the bridge affords a common view of the landscape and helps us see things we could not have seen on either side.

Sampath (Sam) Iyengar
CEO, PSI Data Systems Ltd.
Aditya Birla Group, India

Acknowledgments

A number of people have helped me with this book, either with the manuscript itself or, more often, by providing me with opportunities to work with Indians and Westerners in the thick of the East-West face-off. And I welcome this opportunity to recognize and thank them.

Marty McCaffrey (to whom I gratefully dedicate this book) deserves his own paragraph; he introduced me to and put me in front of numerous Indian and Western businessmen and women from whom I heard countless stories from the trenches, which then became the backbone of this volume.

My good friend Kedar Dwivedi has been my guide to Indian culture and psychology for more than 20 years, answering countless questions I have put to him, in person and by email. Kedar also reviewed the first draft and offered many helpful suggestions and insights. Another good friend, Michael Dowling, formerly with HSBC, has kindly shared his insights with me (about India, among other things) for more than 20 years.

I am also very grateful to Sam Iyengar for writing the Foreword; Sam and I have never met (in this life, anyway), but we share a common passion for "getting the cultural piece right."

Special thanks are owed to a number of folks at Target: Randy Kirihara for bringing me out to Minneapolis in the first place; Patrick Brown for his continued support and great stories about India; Judi Hovde, Mary Texer, and Tom Slover for their support of dozens of workshops over the years.

At ABN AMRO I would like to thank Mike Siconolfi, Tamara Tannen, Monica Rodriguez, and Arkeelaus Sherman; at Best Buy, Bruce Mielke; at Chase, Vishy Vishwanathan and Duane Baggerley; at CNA, Chris Gilmore; at Key Bank Ravi Alangar; at MetLife, Paul Malchow and Sammy Rushing; at New York Life, Carol Faiella; at SunTrust, Paul McDonough and Theresa Mahecha; at World Learning, Jim Blake; at Pfizer, Bill Tavenor; and at National City Bank, Carla Lyons, Chris Lynn, and Stacey McCauley.

And on the Indian side thanks to: Ranjini Manian of Global Adjustments, Jitin Eidnani at Cognizant, Vikas Goyal at Wipro, and Bill Thomas at Tata.

And on the home front, my wife Charlotte, as always, kept the world at bay so I could sit at my computer with nothing to worry about except where the words were going to come from. Thank you, C.

Introduction: "The Worm Has Turned"

Over the next few years you will see a dramatic gap opening between countries. It will be between those who get it and are fully mobilized in China and India and those that are still pondering.
Jim Hemerling
The Boston Consulting Group

No big international company can do without an India strategy.
The Economist

In the past decade, millions of people around the world, especially in the West, have discovered India. People who have never been to India, who will never go to India, and who until recently had never heard of places like Pune, Gurgaon, and Hyderabad—these same people now talk or exchange e-mails several times a day with colleagues in India or with colleagues from India in their own workplace. Many more, who do not have daily contact, participate in weekly conference calls and regular reviews and updates. Meanwhile, several million Indians who have never heard of Pittsburgh, Guelph, and Hampstead are likewise now in daily contact with people in those odd-sounding locales.

All in the name of . . . well, actually the name varies depending on the nature of the collaboration between the Western company and its Indian counterpart; it might be outsourcing, strategic sourcing, off-shoring, following the sun, strategic partnering, a joint venture, or captive operations. Whatever it is called, for most people it boils down to having contact on a regular basis with colleagues from another hemisphere and, so far as culture is concerned, from a different world.

Offshore Is in Your Future

By almost any measure, the contact between East and West is only going to increase. *Business Week* predicts outsourcing to India will quadruple by 2010. "India now appears on every corporate to-do list," *The Economist* noted recently.

By almost any measure, the contact between East and West is only going to increase.

Even in the furnace of pre-monsoonal heat, linen-suited Westerners (and Easterners) are appearing in Mumbai, Bangalore, and Chennai anxious not to miss out. Indian business has secured a niche in the world economy that can only grow in importance. The question is no longer whether India can fly, but how high." ("Can India Fly?," 2006)

By *any* measure? A look at some key indicators does indeed suggest that what has already been a remarkably fast-growing business phenomenon is poised to grow even faster. Not all the growth will be in India, of course, but the numbers suggest that India will more than hold its own in the coming global competition in information technology (IT), business process outsourcing (BPO), and a growing number of other sectors. Here are some figures

Information Technology

- Global spending on IT outsourcing is projected to grow from $150 billion in 2000 to $250 billion in 2008 ("Men and machines," 2004).
- Indian IT industry revenue grew 32 percent in 2004 to $22 billion and is projected to reach $148 billion by 2012 (Hamm, 2005).

- India currently has two-thirds of the global market in offshore IT services and half of that in BPO ("Can India Fly?," 2006).
- Nearly "68 percent of India's exported IT and IT-enabled services are headed for the United States." (Daniel, 2007)
- The productivity growth of India's IT services is the highest in the world ("Faster, Cheaper, Better," 2004).

Business Process Outsourcing

- Global spending on Business Process Outsourcing (BPO) is projected to grow from $100 billion in 2000 to $175 billion in 2008 ("Men and machines," 2004).
- Indian BPO revenue grew 40 percent to $5.8 billion in 2004 and is projected to hit $64 billion and employ 3 million people by 2012 (Hamm, 2005).

IT and BPO Combined

- In 2005 BPO and IT revenues combined accounted for 5 percent of India's entire GDP, and they are expected to contribute 7 percent of GDP—and account for 17 percent of all growth—by 2010 ("Virtual Champions," 2006).
- In 2006 the three largest Indian companies involved in offshore ventures—Tata Consulting Services, Infosys, and Wipro—increased their revenues by 36 percent, 35 percent, and 30 percent respectively ("Virtual Champions," 2006).

Other

- India has 28 percent of the available supply of qualified labor in lowcost countries ("If in Doubt," 2006).
- Twenty-three percent of the increase in the world's working age population over the next five years will be in India.
- The average salary of an Indian IT engineer is $5,000; an industrial engineer makes $390 a month ("If in Doubt," 2006).

- A graduate with a master's degree in business makes $7,500 a year (or one tenth of the U.S. equivalent) ("If in Doubt," 2006).
- Over 16 percent of all the work done by the world's IT services industry is being carried out remotely from where the services are consumed ("World of Work," 2004).

"India has always been seen as a country of promise and potential," notes Mamdan Nilekani, CEO of Infosys, "but it has not delivered. Now even long-term skeptics are being converted: The worm has turned" ("Now for the Hard Part," 2006).

Not Just IT

But the stampede to India has not been limited to IT and BPO; almost every day brings news of new sectors and new specialties within existing sectors where Western companies are partnering with Indians. "Think of any job that can be done remotely, by computer or telephone," Steve Hamm wrote recently in *Business Week*, "and you're looking at a job that can be done by an Indian" (Hamm, 2005). Two economists at the Institute for International Economics in Washington echo this sentiment in their study of U.S. service jobs. Jensen and Kletzer calculated how many people in the American workforce work at a distance from their customers, "figuring that if their jobs can de done at, say, 200 miles from the customer, they could almost as easily be done half a world away by people in Shanghai or Bangalore. By the distance criterion, they calculate that half of U.S. jobs are in occupations or industries that are 'tradable'" (Coy, 2005).

A list of just some of the tasks currently being done offshore in India includes:

Banking/financial services: loan applications, credit reports, brokerage services, credit card customer support, credit card fraud detection, equities analysis and research, market research—and in the hedge funds sector: reconciling trades, valuing investments, and demand planning

Insurance: applications processing, claims processing and administration, policy underwriting, customer service

Legal services: drafting patent filings, case research, contract and loan documentation, litigation support

Mortgage services: application processing, cashflow projections, commercial property market research and analysis, customer service

Television: digitization, video-editing, captioning

Newspapers: editorial services, graphic design, ad production

Medicine: radiological services (reading CT scans and X-rays), transcribing physicians' notes

Pharmaceuticals: research, drug trials, drug discovery software

Airlines: reservations, baggage tracking, in-flight entertainment technology

And then there are the decidedly niche markets: Smarthinking, a Washington, DC-based math and science tutoring service, has 80 tutors taking calls in India. Anirudh Phadke, owner of another tutoring firm, the New Delhi-based Career Launcher, says he was initially worried that U.S. students might balk at the idea of overseas tutors, but he quickly found that "they don't really care about where we are" (Toppo, 2005).

As *Business Week* noted recently, the kind of work moving offshore is no longer just the labor-intensive, repetitive, low-end technological grunt work of the past (the data-entry paradigm), but now includes more complicated tasks such as the design and testing of sophisticated, high-end products, requiring complex and innovative technological solutions.

Wipro, Ittiam, HCL Technologies, and others are bringing together chips, circuit boards, embedded software, and industrial design—the whole stack of skills and technology needed to create a finished product. That can shave months and even years off product developments, a godsend for Western companies under great pressure to cut costs.

Bangalore's HCL designed a backup navigation system for the Airbus A340 and A320 jetliners in just 18 months.

> Working from digital prototypes, [Tata's] 850-engineer center in Bangalore is helping a U.S. automaker design the drive engine, outer body, and interior layout of a future passenger car. For a leading developer of orthopedic implants, Tata's engineers analyze CAT scans and custom-design replacement hips, knees, and wrist bones to fit patients awaiting surgery in American hospitals. For other U.S. clients TCS has helped develop a forklift, a small earthmover, a golf cart, and high-security locks. (Hamm, 2005)

These developments are sometimes referred to as the second or even third generation of the India boom. "We came to India for the costs," Dan Scheinman, Cisco Systems vice-president for corporate development has observed, "we stayed for the quality, and now we're investing for the innovation" (Engardio, 2005).

"We came to India for the costs, we stayed for the quality, and now we're investing for the innovation." —Dan Scheinman, Cisco Systems

---

MBA students from the United States and Europe are passing up summer internships on Wall Street or at the FTSE in London and going to India, where they figure they can learn something even more useful for their careers. "I can't help but feel that I am witnessing the creation of a new global economic order," one Western intern at Hewlitt-Packard India observed, " a new reality that most people back home don't realize is coming" (Rai, 2005).

The India boom is making it hard for Indian companies to find enough qualified workers. Ten years ago one of the biggest players in the IT arena, Infosys, "hired 90 percent of its new employees from the top tier of Indian universities," *The New York Times* reported recently. Today it has to be satisfied with 10 percent and has to cast its recruiting net much wider to include nearly 200 Indian colleges (Norris, 2007). Indeed, a number of Indian companies are now opening their own institutions to train the candidates they can no longer find in the marketplace.

Not only is the type of work taking place in India becoming increasingly diverse, the kind of company embracing the offshore model is also evolving. The offshore charge was led and for some time restricted to first tier, billion-dollar players: the biggest banks, the leading insurance companies, the Fortune 500's, and the FTSE 100's. Increasingly, more and more mid-sized companies in Europe and America have begun doing the math and realize that significant cost savings can be had even at their level. And these companies are being vigorously courted, meanwhile, by second-tier (and even some first-tier) Indian vendors who have figured out how to make the economics of outsourcing work for thousands of mid-market players. As mid-sized companies climb on the India bandwagon, the number of Westerners who will be interacting with Indians is poised to grow exponentially.

While the majority of Westerners interacting with Indians will do so in some form of the offshore model, those whose companies and organizations have no projects in India—and no prospects for any—may still find themselves sharing the workplace with folks from the subcontinent. There are over 20 million people in the Indian diaspora, mainly in the West, with 2 million in the United States. In California alone there are over 3,000 companies owned by Indians. Indians make up a large percentage of the immigrant population in the United Kingdom and its former colonies, and Indian students attend colleges and universities throughout the Western world, including 80,000 in the United States (the most of any foreign country) (Kamdar, 2007).

The Cultural Component

Clearly the meeting of India and the West—and the coming together in the workplace of Indians and Westerners—is accelerating, with no downturn visible in the immediate future, although many multinationals are already looking to China as "the next big thing" in offshore partnering. (But even then, it should be noted, a lot of the work being done for

Western multinationals in China is subcontracted out of India.) A growing number of Americans and Europeans now interact on a daily or weekly basis—whether by phone, e-mail, or face–to face—with colleagues in India, with Indian colleagues in their own workplace, or both. And the same is true in reverse for Indians. And many other Indians and Westerners have occasional contact with each other, have indirect responsibility for various aspects of an offshore venture, or manage employees with direct and frequent contact with foreign counterparts. This book has been written for all those involved in any way in the offshore experience who have contact with or need to better understand colleagues from the other side of the world.

And why might Indians and Westerners need a book to tell them how to understand each other? The short answer is that people from different cultures have different values and beliefs, and these sometimes cause them to behave differently in various situations. These unexpected and surprising behaviors in turn lead to confusion, frustration, and even offense, which then result in growing mistrust and a gradual breakdown in communications. Working relations deteriorate, the partnership is undermined, and the entire operation is imperiled.

That's the short answer as to why Indians and Westerners need to understand each other better. For the long answer, turn to chapter 1.

Indians, Westerners, and the Cultural Lens

What I say is this [the Indian man remarked] and this I do not say to all Englishmen: God made us different, you and I, and your fathers and my fathers. For one thing, we have not the same notions of honesty and speaking the truth. That is not our fault, because we are made so. And look now what you do? You come and judge us by your own standards of morality. You are, of course, too hard on us. And again I tell you: you are great fools in this matter. Who are we to have your morals, or you to have ours?

Rudyard Kipling
"East and West"

The portion we see of human beings is very small. Their forms and faces, voices and words . . . [But] beyond these, like an immense dark continent, lies all that has made them.

Freya Stark
The Journey's Echo

Cultural differences like the ones described in this book have been implicated in many of the frustrations, inefficiencies, and, in some cases, the actual failure of Indian-Western partnerships and joint ventures. According to industry experts at Gartner, half of all outsourcing ventures fail, and while cultural differences alone do not usually cause these failures, they are quite often a major contributing factor. Those ventures that do succeed often do so *in spite of* cultural problems. How much better it would be if these ventures could be even more successful—and succeed even sooner—if the cultural problems could be identified and eliminated at the outset.

Those ventures that do succeed often do so *in spite of* cultural problems.

Cultural differences have repeatedly been found to play a significant role in the following problems that affect many offshore ventures:

- Delayed rollout
- Unrealized/smaller than expected cost savings
- Unsuccessful/slower than expected knowledge transfer
- Too much time managing the relationship
- Production delays
- Missed deadlines
- Work that has to be redone
- Backlash against outsourcing from the company's workforce ("We told you so")

Fixing the cultural piece will not cause these problems to go away, but it will mitigate many of them and, more important, create the circumstances—mutual understanding and trust—that will enable all those involved to put in place the other measures that sooner or later *will* send these problems packing.

Which Westerners?

Before we go any further, we should probably be more precise about these Westerners we've being going on about. Can we really make meaningful statements about such a large and diverse group? Jacques Barzun, for one, doesn't think so: "Of all the books that no one can write," he has observed, "those about nations and the national character are the most impossible" (Kammen 1980, xvii). Bloody but unbowed, we actually propose to go Barzun one better and write a book about an entire *group* of nations. If it's impossible to write meaningfully about one country, then surely it is close to madness to write about a collection of countries.

In our defense, we have pared down what we mean by Western countries in these pages to include only the following: the United States, northern Europe (in particular the United Kingdom but also the Netherlands, Germany, and the Scandinavian countries), and the former British colonies of Canada, Australia, and New Zealand. (The latter two are not geographically in the West, of course, but their cultures are certainly more Western, specifically more British, than they are Asian.) We do *not* include any other Western European countries in our definition, most especially not southern, Mediterranean, or what might be called Latin Europe. This region is indisputably part of the West, but the cultures of Mediterranean Europe are quite different from those of northern Europe. Most generalizations we can safely make about northern Europe and the United States, therefore, do not apply to southern Europe. When we speak of the West, Westerners, and Western countries in these pages, we mean the United States, northern Europe, and the former British colonies (except where otherwise indicated).

The reader may still wonder how we can get away with lumping Germany, say, in the same cultural bloc as England or the United States. The answer is that with respect to the cultural issues that come up the most often in the offshore experience, namely communication style and management style, the Western countries are similar to each other in their overall assumptions and values, if not always in the specific applications of those assumptions. Managers in both Germany and the United States, for example, delegate authority and expect subordinates to make independent decisions, but German managers typically expect to be kept better informed about such decisions than their American counterparts.

Moreover, for all the subtle—and even not so subtle—cultural differences among the various Western countries in communication and management style, the overall approach in each country is much closer to that of the other Western countries than it is to that of India.

Which Indians?

In some ways it's even harder to write about the single country of India than it is to write about all the Western countries described above. Winston Churchill is reputed to have said that India is no more a country than is the equator. And he is in good company, for the overwhelming consensus is that there's no such place as India—and, by extension, no such thing as an Indian. Westerners will tell you this; Indians will tell you this; and the facts will tell you this. Amaryta Sen, India's Nobel laureate in economics, is fond of quoting one of his Western teachers, who told him: "Whatever you can rightly say about India, the opposite is also true" (2005, 137).

"The simple fact is that we are all minorities in India," Shashi Tharoor writes in his book *India: From Midnight to the Millenium and Beyond.* "There has never been an archetypal Indian to stand alongside the archetypal Englishman or Frenchman" (1997). Just one look at the religious, racial, ethnic, geographic, linguistic, class, caste, and socioeconomic diversity of India is enough to confirm Tharoor's view, and should be more than enough to scare off any would-be pontificators. It has not frightened anyone, of course (present company included), but it has instilled in all of us a generous dose of humility.

Almost all nations celebrate their diversity, but none with more justification than India. There is north India and south India; east India and west India; Hindu, Moslem, Sikh, and Jain India; desert India, tropical India, and Himalayan India; urban India and rural India; very rich India and dirt-poor India; modern India and traditional India. In any book or article about India it's not possible to get past the second or third page or the first few paragraphs before running across the obligatory land-of-contrasts passage, explaining why the country is fundamentally unprofileable. "This is a country where 300 million people live in absolute poverty," one recent example reads

> Most of them in its 680,000 villages, but where cell phone users have jumped from 3 million in 2000 to 100 million in 2005, and the number of television channels from 1 in 1991 to more than 150 last year.
>
> India's economy has grown by 6 percent annually since 1991, a rate exceeded only by China's, yet there are a mere 35 million taxpayers in a country with a population of 1.1 billion. Only 10 percent of India's workers have jobs in the formal economy. Its excellent engineering schools turn out a million graduates each year, 10 times the number for the United States and Europe combined, yet 35 percent of the country remains illiterate. (Grimes, 2007)

Fortunately, we plan to describe only a small subset of Indians in these pages—educated urban professionals—who, while they come from all the different Indias, share a common subculture that makes them more like each other than like the Indians of their various homelands. Indeed, in many ways they have more in common with urban professionals in London and Los Angeles than with the bullock-cart drivers they drive past while commuting to downtown Bangalore.

About these Indians it is possible to make accurate and useful generalizations, so long as one remembers the first rule of all generalizations: they must be taken with a grain of salt (including those about the West). Generalizations are only true *in general*; they may be accurate about a group but not necessarily about any individual member of that group or for any particular set of circumstances. You will never meet a general person, in other words, and you will never be in a general situation. In the end, you have to deal with the person standing in front of you, who in some respects may indeed be just like the general Indian or the general American you have read about in books like this, but who in other ways will be nothing like the stereotype. That doesn't make them wrong—most stereotypes contain at least a germ of truth—but it does make such stereotypes incomplete and potentially misleading.

Two Types of Indians

Even within the narrow subset of Indians we will describe in these pages, there is an important distinction that needs to be made between those who have spent some time in the West and those who have not. The former, obviously, are somewhat or even very familiar with Western ways, while all the latter know about the West is what they have heard (chiefly from other Indians).

Why is this important? If, as an American or European, you are dealing with an Indian who is living in your country and working in your workplace, or who may be back in India but previously sojourned in your country, you can reasonably assume that that individual understands some things about your culture, certainly more than an Indian who has never been to your country. This Indian, let's call him Raj, has worked with and alongside Americans or the English, let's say, has observed how they interact with each other, and knows, therefore, how—ethnocentric as we all are—these Americans or Brits expect him to behave: just like them.

Raj, who is also ethnocentric—or was up until now—begins to notice that a lot of the ways he has always behaved, which he thought of as right and normal back home, are nowhere to be seen in Boston or Birmingham; indeed, when he behaves in those ways people look at him strangely, or worse. As a result, Raj begins to adjust his behavior to be more like what he sees around him every day in the workplace, for that behavior, strange as it appears to him, is clearly normal and appropriate in this environment. Raj, in short, is becoming Westernized, and because he is becoming Westernized, Westerners are finding it increasingly easy to understand and work with him.

Raj will never become completely Westernized, of course; he will most likely adopt Western behaviors in some circumstances but not others and will typically revert to "type" (his Indian self) when he is under a lot of pressure. In other words, while Westerners can reasonably expect fewer cultural misunderstandings with Westernized Indians like Raj, they should still be careful not to mistake a few outward trappings of Western behavior for a complete personality change.

Just how Western a Westernized Indian actually becomes depends on a number of factors: how long the Indian has worked in the Indian business culture (how *Easternized* he or she is); how old he or she is (younger Indians tend to be more flexible and adaptable); who the Indian actually reports to (whether he or she reports to an Indian boss in the United States or the United Kingdom or to a Western boss); how long the Indian spends in the West; and whether he or she comes alone (in which case they tend to adapt more quickly) or with a group of Indians (with whom the Indian may interact as much or even more than with the Westerners in the workplace).

The second type of Indian is someone who has not spent any time or spent very little time in the West. This person, let's call her Sumitra, has not seen Americans or Brits in action on their cultural turf, has not observed how they interact with each other in the workplace, does not realize how they are expecting her to behave—like them—and does not understand, therefore, that the way she in fact behaves is not always appropriate, normal, or understood in the West. Sumitra does not adjust her behavior, does not become Westernized, and is not as easy for Westerners to understand and work with. For obvious reasons, Americans and Europeans will have more cultural problems with Sumitra, most likely some of the very problems described in the rest of this book.

Even Westerners who understand all this sometimes hold out the hope that as time goes by and she has more contact with the West, Sumitra, even without the benefit of a stay in Minneapolis or Manchester, will somehow become a little more Westernized. A little, perhaps, but Westerners must remember that the Western workplace has no immediacy or reality for Sumitra, no real claim on her, no matter how much time she spends on the phone with Americans, how many conference calls she sits in on, or how many e-mails she writes. The Indian workplace, meanwhile, is immediate and very real; her future depends on her succeeding in that environment, not in Minneapolis. Indeed, if Sumitra *were* to become Westernized, it would not do anything for her career.

On this same note we might mention what often happens to our friend Raj when he goes back to India after an extended stint in Cleveland. If he has in fact morphed into a Westernized Indian, then there's every chance his homecoming will be rocky. Typically, he would have to shed some of his new Western behaviors in order to fit back into the Indian workplace. Meanwhile, his Western colleagues back in Cleveland with whom he still works know nothing of this new Raj (who is actually the old Raj) and don't understand why he has suddenly "gone Indian" on them.

The Culture Thing

These, then, are the Westerners and the Indians we'll be describing in these pages. Now we need to take up another fundamental question: Is the Western-Indian cultural divide really so wide that it takes an entire book to explain it? We read the newspapers and the weekly newsmagazines; we get the international news; we know all about globalization, one world, the shrinking planet, and the worldwide Web. We know there are other cultures, that other people aren't like us, and that we're not like them. We get the culture thing. So where's the problem?

Many people do in fact "get the culture thing," in the sense that they have some general awareness of cultural differences, especially in Europe, where there is routine contact between people from different cultures. This is less true of Americans, however, who typically (or at least *stereo-typically*) are not as wise to the ways of culture, given their cultural isolation and relative lack of exposure.

But the truth is that people in both groups, including, incidentally, the British—who ought to "get" Indians if anyone should—people in both groups, for all of their awareness, still react to and get upset by the weird things foreigners do. Awareness of cultural differences, in short, only gets you so far in the cultural sweepstakes.

We Are All Ethnocentrics

Why isn't awareness enough to make the cultural problems go away? The answer is that awareness of culture is in the mind, while reaction to culture is in the emotions—and when has logic ever defeated feelings in a fair fight? Merely knowing something to be true, such as those who understand culture can be said to, and *acting* as if it were true are two very different phenomena. "There is all the difference in the world," Aldous Huxley writes, "between believing academically, with the intellect, and believing personally, intimately, with the whole living self." (1985, 207)

To understand all this better, we need to take a short detour through the subject of cultural conditioning, the process by which people become "ethnocentric," by which they learn to regard the way they behave as normal and natural and all other ways of behaving as abnormal and unnatural. Cultural conditioning, in other words, explains one of the great truths of human nature: most people expect most other people to behave like themselves, *including people who come from foreign cultures.* This isn't rational, of course, as we noted above, but then another great truth of human nature is that people don't always behave rationally—and a very good thing that is, too, as we will soon see.

But why do people, against all reason and logic, expect other people to behave like them? Simply stated: because they always have. Most of us are born to, raised by, and grow up surrounded by people of our same "type"—people of our same nationality, our same race (usually), our same ethnic group, our same religion, and our same socioeconomic group. We may come into occasional contact with people of distinctly different types, and we may even have some friends and colleagues of this sort, but the truth is most of us have our most frequent, significant interactions with other people like us, with people, in short, who think and behave largely the way we do.

This is where we get our expectation that other people will behave like us, or, as we sometimes say, that they will behave "normally." But we do not merely *expect* other people to behave normally; we *require* it. The deep conviction that other people will behave like us, that they will be aware of and adhere to the agreed-upon norms of our particular group or society, is what makes most human interaction possible. If we did not know—indeed, if we could not be absolutely certain—that people would behave in predictable ways in all manner of situations, we would be afraid to leave our houses in the morning or even to get out of bed. "We are all subject in our thinking . . . to ethnocentrism," Hickson and Pugh have written. "This is the implicit assumption, often unawares, that our culture is the best, that our way of doing things is normal, the right way . . . . *The development of this belief in our own culture is an important part of our ability to function effectively in it*" (italics added) (1995, 253–54).

But this undeniably handy feature of human nature does cause a few problems when we encounter people *who are not like us*, people from other cultures, for example, such as India or the United States. Raised with a different set of norms, they don't always behave the way we do, but since we are expecting them to—indeed, since we are *depending on* them to—even though we may "know" better, the stage is set for surprise, confusion, and a great deal of frustration. When Indians and Westerners work together, then, everyone behaving perfectly normally as each defines it, each side in fact often finds the behavior of the other *ab*normal. "When we see something different in another [society]," Hickson and Pugh continue, "we are liable to view it as abnormal and inferior . . . a feature of human nature which does lead to problems when we come to operate in other cultures" (254).

When Indians and Westerners work together, everyone behaving perfectly normally as they define it, each side in fact often finds the behavior of the other quite *ab*normal.

Needless to say, when people start finding the behavior of other people they regularly work with to be abnormal, unpredictable, and incomprehensible, relations can quickly deteriorate, with all manner of unpleasant consequences for the work they're trying to do together. And that, in a nutshell, is why culture matters.

When people find the behavior of other people they work with abnormal, unpredictable, and incomprehensible, relations can quickly deteriorate.

The solution to the cultural mismatch between expectations and behavior is twofold: Indians and Westerners can become better informed about each other's norms and adjust their expectations to be more in line with how people from the other culture actually behave. Or each side can change its behaviors to be more in line with what people from the other culture are expecting. Both approaches help break down ethnocentrism and reduce the surprise, confusion, and frustration built into most cross-cultural interactions. And both depend on the kind of cultural information presented in the remaining chapters of this book.

But We Get Cultural Training

Many Indian vendors provide cultural training for their employees, especially for those who are going to the West but also for those who remain in India but who will regularly interact by phone or e-mail with Western colleagues. Both Indians and Westerners often feel that this type of training has been sufficient to, in effect, turn Sumitra into Raj. This is an unwarranted and unfortunate assumption; unwarranted because it is manifestly not true, and unfortunate because those who think it is true, whether they're Indians or Westerners, mistakenly believe that thanks to such training they have dodged the cultural bullet. When they discover later they have not, the consequences can be all the more serious for being completely unexpected.

First, the truth part. While cultural training is necessary and beneficial, in most cases it only raises awareness, and as we have already seen in this chapter, awareness gets you into the game, but it doesn't guarantee you'll be a winner. Much of so-called cultural training is not in fact cultural, dealing with differences in values and behavior, but "country" training, facts about the target country, such as the names of regional sports teams or popular television programs and lists of do's and don'ts. The latter are valuable, incidentally—we have such a list in chapter 10— but mastering do's and don'ts is a little like memorizing the script but not knowing which act it is.

The danger of cultural training for Indians is the false sense of security it may give them, whereby they believe themselves to be much more culturally adept than they in fact are. The real cultural problems—such as when Indians and Westerners misinterpret each other's communications— are not going to go away just because you remember to use deodorant every day or to call your boss by her first name. The danger for Americans and Europeans is in assuming that thanks to cultural training the Indians they work with have become Westernized and won't cause any cultural problems.

None of this is meant to denigrate training; there should be more of it, and on both sides of the cultural divide. Westerners who are in a client-vendor relationship with Indians often feel that it is just the Indians who should get training. However, because the cultural misunderstandings are mutual, both sides need to work at bridging the gap. If Indians build a bridge from their side and Westerners a bridge from theirs, the bridge gets finished a lot faster. Training is also valuable for another reason that has nothing to do with the content but with the message it sends: if they're sending us to training, then this culture stuff must be important.

It's Not *Always* Culture

We should be careful meanwhile not to overstate the role culture plays in behavior. What we have called culture—people's values, beliefs, and assumptions—is indeed a major influence on the things they say and do, but it is almost never the whole story, nor even always the most important part of the story. What happens in any given interaction between two or more individuals is the result of numerous causes, from the sublime (such as values) to the very mundane (whether the person slept well the night before) to everything in between (how well the people know each other, how they're getting along today, who else is present, whether either of them is in a hurry, age differences, gender differences, the weather, time of day, and so on).

In other words, readers are cautioned not to assume that once they understand the Western culture or the Indian culture, they will be able to predict with certainty what the Westerner or the Indian is going to do in most situations. Culture *is* a piece of the puzzle, and it's certainly better to have that piece than not to have it, but it's not the whole picture. At the same time, we should also point out that not every misunderstanding between an Indian and a Westerner is automatically a cultural misunderstanding. Cultural differences are always a *potential* explanation for any misunderstanding between an Indian and a Westerner, but they are not the only explanation. Two Indians or two Westerners don't always understand each other either, yet they come from the same culture.

The Public and Private Sectors

Another caveat we need to make is that there is a big difference in India between workplace attitudes and behaviors in the public or government sector—the vaunted ICS (Indian Civil Service)—and in the private sector. For one thing, there is much more job security in the former and less of a need, therefore, to worry about ingratiating oneself with one's boss or otherwise being careful to always defer to and never confront higher-ups (see chapter 3). For another, there is much less experimentation and innovation in the public sector, which tends to be much more traditional, bureaucratic, and resistant to change.

In these pages we describe the private sector workplace, especially the information technology and business process outsourcing sectors, which comprise the heart of India's offshore boom. These sectors are relatively new, no more than two decades old, and in some ways possess quite unique business cultures.

Fooled By Appearances

First-timers to India may be surprised at how familiar everything looks and may wonder, therefore, where all this talk about cultural differences is coming from. Shopping malls and even certain streets in Mumbai, Bangalore, New Delhi, and other booming cities look a lot like those in any major city in the West. All the brands are there, too: Starbucks, KFC, NIKE, Abercrombie & Fitch, Toys "R" Us, Mercedes and BMW, Apple and SONY. And a lot of the Indians you meet dress just like the folks back home, download the same music to their iPods, go to many of the same movies, and watch many of the same television shows. Moreover, the offices and office buildings Indians work in could be anywhere in the modern, western world. Add to this the fact that many of the Indians one meets speak excellent—and sometimes even idiomatic—English, and it's no wonder Americans and Europeans begin to think India is really just like back home, only with better weather. "Most Indians . . . speak English well," Gunjan Bagla of the consulting firm Amritt ventures has observed, "so it is not uncommon to underestimate cultural differences." (Daniel)

But Westerners should resist the temptation. The part of culture that really matters, the part that causes the misunderstandings and confusion chronicled in these pages, is not visible; it lies beneath the surface in people's values, beliefs, and, most importantly, in their underlying assumptions or worldview—most of which are learned in the home in the first two decades of life. (See chapter 2.) Indians may go to work every day in a reasonable facsimile of the West, but they go home every night to India.

"This is one of the most significant learnings I have taken away from all my long visits to India," an American corporate executive told this writer in a recent e-mail:

> Because of the strong English language skills of so many of the younger people we are working with, it's easy to get lulled to sleep and [forget] that there are indeed significant cultural differences. The Bangalore office may have all of the corporate US trappings, but when they go out the door at 7:00 PM, the Indians are immediately back in the swirling curry of India as soon as they leave the guarded parking lot or step onto a bus.

The arms of the collectivist ingroup is what they go home to each night and weekend, where they share stories about the companies they work for with immediate and extended family. While they may appreciate and enjoy the office and its western culture, they are more importantly *obliged, indebted, and beholden* to their Indian ingroup. The traditional ingroup values are the ones that will be reinforced in the most significant ways and remain the most influential.

When all is said and done, an Indian who eats lunch at Pizza Hut every day is not an American; he's an Indian with a taste for pizza.

Indians from a Western Perspective

It's almost certain that many Indians will not recognize themselves in these pages, and for a very good reason: this book is not about how Indians see themselves. It is, rather, about how Indians are perceived by Westerners. All the issues discussed here surface repeatedly in interviews and conversations with professionals in the West who work with people from or in India; indeed, these issues were part of the inspiration for this book. But these perceptions are not always accurate or correct, just as Indian perceptions of Westerners would not always be accurate. Indeed, how Westerners see Indians is quite often *in*accurate, as we are at great pains to point out elsewhere in the text. But inaccurate perceptions make just as much of an impact as accurate ones, if not more.

A Focus on the Workplace

All appearances notwithstanding, this is not a book about Indian culture—about the customs, history, politics, and geography of the subcontinent. And a good thing that is, too, for while I have spent a considerable amount of time in India, worked with many Indians, and interviewed scores more for this project, I am not an expert on India and make no such claim. What this book *is* about, and where I can claim some expertise, is key differences in workplace values, attitudes, and behaviors between people from India and people from the United States and northern Europe.

When you finish this book, then, if you're from a Western country, you still won't know the color of mourning, the capital of Rajasthan, or why Sikh men wear turbans,* but you should understand your Indian colleagues much better. And if you're Indian, then you will understand better how you are seen by your Western colleagues.

But enough context. Let's go to the workplace, meet some real Indians and real Westerners, and see what all the fuss is about.

---

*Though you will if you read footnotes. The color of mourning is white; Jaipur is the capital of Rajasthan; and traditional Sikh men wear turbans because they never cut their hair.

Communication East and Communication West

No institution in India is more important than the family. [It is] more important than the individual at one end of society's spectrum or the nation at the other.

Stanley Wolpert
India

The Eastern emphasis on self-regulation of emotion, empathy, and avoiding hurting others' feelings requires [the] development of a style that places more value on indirect, hypothetical, and metaphorical communication, turning it into an art form.

Kedar Dwivedi

A client once told me the following story.

An American (let's call him Bill) who works in the IT division of a major retail chain was overseeing the creation of a new software application being developed by a team of Indian programmers. One month into the project, the original completion date for the application was moved forward by six weeks, as Bill explained to the onshore Indian team lead (Deepak) at their next weekly update meeting. Bill asked Deepak if this would cause any problems, and Deepak said it "probably wouldn't."

At the end of that meeting, Deepak announced he was getting married in a few months and invited Bill and his wife to the wedding. At each successive weekly update, the two men talked about the application, and then, at the end of each meeting, Deepak filled Bill in on how the wedding plans were going, including problems with the usual things like finding a venue, deciding whom to invite, and having to reprint the announcements because the date was wrong.

The wedding was going to take place in India, and Bill had made it clear from the beginning that he and his wife would not be able to attend. But he was touched that Deepak shared with him all the planning details and even asked for Bill's advice from time to time.

Like many Westerners, Bill had no idea what Deepak was actually trying to tell him (he only realized much later), and like many Indians, Deepak assumed Bill had understand him.

Misunderstandings like these are daily occurrences in the workplace and the source of more of the confusion, frustration, and general hair-pulling accompanying the East-West interface than any other single factor. Over time—and it doesn't take long—these incidents of miscommunication begin to erode trust between the two sides, undermining interpersonal relations and ultimately jeopardizing the entire collaboration. Since communication is at the core of most workplace interactions, the potential for any *mis*communication is automatically a very serious matter, and that potential is always higher when the workers in question come from different cultures.

So we will begin our look at Indian-Western cultural differences with the subject of communication. In this chapter we give an overview of the origin of the Indian and Western styles of communication, to be followed in chapter 3 by a detailed analysis of the most common kinds of East-West misunderstandings along with specific and practical advice about how to avoid them.

Communication East: For the Good of the Group

Like all other human behavior, communication—how people send and receive messages—is greatly influenced by culture, that is, by the deep-seated values and beliefs that are the ultimate source of all our actions. And the one aspect of culture that accounts for more miscommunication between Indians and Westerners than any other is what is usually called the concept of identity. Simply stated, Indians are more group-oriented (collectivist), and Westerners, especially Americans, are more individual-oriented (individualist). And this is not a match made in heaven.

What does it mean to be group-oriented and exactly how does this affect the way Indians communicate? People who are group-oriented identify first and foremost with their group—their family, extended family, a team at work—and only secondarily with their "self." They are raised to put the desires and needs of the group (also known as their "ingroup") ahead of their own personal needs. This doesn't mean Indians don't have individual aspirations or desires—although traditional religion did teach that the self or ego was considered "either unreal or displeasing to God"—but rather that they have been conditioned to identify their own good as inseparably linked with the good of others—so much so, in fact, that many Indians would not make a meaningful distinction between the two (Lannoy, 112). In such a scheme, the survival and well-being of the individual are effectively synonymous with the survival and well-being of the group.

An American told me the story of a group of 18 young Indians who were brought to Minneapolis for some training at the home office of their company. The Indians actually belonged to three different teams of six programmers, each reporting to a different American team leader for the duration of their training. They all trained together in the morning, and then in the afternoon they reported to their respective team leaders to work on different projects. Early one evening the American leader of one of the teams bought pizza for her six programmers, as they were going to have to work through the dinner hour, but they became visibly uncomfortable and politely declined to eat it. When the American inquired why, she discovered that her six Indians were embarrassed to eat the pizza in front of the 12 other Indians—their group—for whom no food was being provided.

The Extended Family

Until very recently, most Indians grew up in an extended family, a multigenerational environment where they were surrounded—and to a large extent raised—by an extensive network of adults: parents, aunts and uncles, grandparents, older brothers, sisters, and cousins. And this is still true for a majority of Indians today. Among other things, the extended family system is a practical necessity for many Indians because of widespread unemployment and the absence of any kind of government welfare or safety net; when Indians are in need, they have to depend on family members for survival.

In extended families, members out of necessity learn how to please and get along with all manner of people with whom they live in very close quarters with virtually no privacy. While young children, especially boys, are often quite indulged in their early years (at least by North American and European standards), after age six or so Indians are expected to listen to, obey, wait upon, and generally defer to anyone who is older. A well-known Indian saying describing the father-son relationship declares that a "son should be treated as a prince for five years, as a slave for ten years, but from his sixteenth birthday, as a friend" (Lannoy 101). After which time, it might be added, he begins to acquire slaves of his own. The extended family may not be quite as ubiquitous as it once was in India, but its influence on Indian behavior, both vestigial and real, is still pervasive.

From an early age, Indians learn how to function within an extensive network of relatives and how to negotiate a web of interdependent relationships replete with duties, obligations, and responsibilities. Among other survival skills, this kind of upbringing teaches Indians to quickly sense and instantly adjust to the moods and feelings of all the significant people they must interact with. Because the extended family system tends to be extremely hierarchical in nature, based mainly on age and to a lesser

extent on gender, Indians also learn how to adjust their behavior according to the status of the person they're dealing with. They learn early on,
for example, to whom they must defer and who must defer to them, from
whom they must seek sufferance and who must seek theirs, to whom they
must make appeals and who must appeal to them, whose support they
depend on and who depends on theirs. "The hierarchical framework is so
pervasive," Jai Sinha has written, "the Indian child internalizes the
process . . . and tends to develop a relative superiority to some and subordination to others. He must protect and take care of those who are inferior to him and maintain deference and respectful compliance with his
superiors" (1990, 35).

Indians learn their place in the pecking order, the place of others, and
the proper way to treat those above and below their station. They learn
how to be patient, obedient, and above all self-effacing. "If all clamored at
once," Stanley Wolpert has written:

> none could be heard nor could the more pressing demands ever
> be met. Indians learn early in life to wait their turn, to be patient.
> Living in and being raised among large families endows Indians
> with a great sense of security and group identity but relatively
> little initiative or what we [Americans] would call rugged indi-
> viduality. There is, indeed, more passivity in Indian personalities
> than we generally find among Americans of comparable age and
> status, a product in great measure of lifelong accommodation to
> the many competing voices, needs, demands, and aspirations of
> the large extended family. (2005, 135)

We might note in passing that the deeply interdependent nature of
Indian society accounts in part for the practice of arranged marriages,
which happens to be one of the most curious and inexplicable aspects
of Indian culture to the Western sensibility. If an individual's survival
and well-being are inseparable from that of the group (the family and
extended family)—if the individual cannot survive emotionally and
psychologically outside the group—then one's chief concern in searching

for a suitable spouse must naturally be whether or not the prospective bride or groom fits into the group. And what better way to guarantee *that* than to have the senior members of the group, parents and other elders, comprise the search committee? Once a candidate suitable to this key constituency has been found, surely the two individuals involved can work out the interpersonal details.

Preserving Harmony and Saving Face

Now that we understand the central place the group occupies in Indian culture, we can complete our short survey of the collectivist mentality by examining the closely related concepts of harmony and face, which, along with loyalty, are arguably the foremost Indian cultural values. Whatever else a group has to do, it has to stay together—all the members have to get along, at least in public—or it is no longer a group. And more than anything else it is harmony, the appearance of agreement and mutual respect, which keeps a group intact.

Because harmony is the glue that holds the group together, preserving harmony becomes the overriding concern in most Indian social and workplace interactions. The need to preserve harmony prescribes a certain code of conduct for all members of the group, namely: being humble and self-effacing, deferring to seniors, avoiding public disagreements and all other kinds of confrontation, never causing offense, and being careful never to embarrass anyone in front of the group. Common to all five of these ideal group behaviors is the underlying necessity to be tuned in and extremely sensitive to the feelings of others—what is usually referred to as the concept of "face."

Most of what is done and not done in Indian society—and especially what is said and not said—comes down to the need to save face.

Most of what is done and not done in Indian society—and especially what is said and not said—comes down to the need to save face, one's own and, even more important, the face of others, in particular one's seniors and elders. Saving face is the driving force behind and the single greatest influence on the Indian style of communication.

What exactly is face? Face is what makes it possible for people to keep their honor and dignity, what saves them from embarrassment, and what preserves their self-respect. Face is perhaps best understood in terms of what causes people in face-saving cultures to lose face. If done in front of other people (such as at a meeting), all of the following have the potential of causing someone else to lose face, the speaker to lose face, or both:

- Openly disagreeing with what someone else says, especially if he or she is senior.
- Correcting what someone else, especially a senior, has said.
- Criticizing someone else who is present.
- Challenging something another person says.
- Making an overtly negative comment about what someone else has said.
- Giving negative feedback.
- Not being able to answer a question one should know the answer to.
- Not being prepared in circumstances where one should be.
- Saying something is not possible.
- Admitting a mistake.
- Admitting one does not know something that one should know.
- Admitting that one does not or did not understand something.
- Admitting that one is not on schedule, is falling behind, is not going to make a deadline.
- Asking for help or for more time.

All these things can be done in Indian society, of course; indeed, they are essential for efficient operations in any workplace. But as far as possible they must be done consistent with the requirements of face, which means they have to be done discretely, politely, and very carefully, which is not a bad three-word summary of the Indian style of communication.

Impact on Communication Style

The collectivist mentality described above, with its core elements of the need to preserve harmony and respect face—to never give offense— explains why Indians talk the way they do. The foremost feature of this style and the defining quality of most conversations between Indians is the overarching necessity to intuit and then say what other people want to hear, thereby preserving good feelings, guaranteeing that no one is embarrassed, and nurturing the all-important group. "Indians like to tell you what you want to hear," Gitanjali Kolanad has observed, "or, rather, what they think you want to hear. The tailor who says it will be ready by Friday and the person who assures you that the place you are looking for is just ahead are obeying a proverb that says 'it is better to say something pleasant than something true'" (2005, 251).

The defining quality of most conversations between Indians is the overarching necessity to say what other people want to hear.

The primary purpose of communication among Indians, in other words, is not to exchange information but rather to preserve harmony and avoid giving offense, thereby safeguarding and strengthening the personal relationship between the speakers. Any information that can be exchanged while respecting this fundamental principle is, of course, most welcome and entirely appropriate in Indian conversation; any information that would violate this principle—for example, anything the other person does *not* want to hear—is unwelcome and inappropriate. Needless to say, this dynamic confines a great deal of critical information to the "not appropriate" category, including all 14 of the items listed above. But while these are indeed things that cannot be *said* among Indians, that does not mean these messages cannot be communicated; it just means they can't be put into words.

So how do Indians communicate all the unpleasant messages people have to express from time to time—all those messages that threaten harmony and undermine face—the messages, in short, that their collectivist society doesn't allow Indians to put into words? In general, Indians express difficult messages in two ways: by what they do *not* say and by what they *don't quite* say, for example, by implying, hinting, or suggesting rather than by being explicit.

What Is Not Said

For the reasons we have already examined, the expectation that people will say what other people want to hear—that they will agree with you, for example, that they are going to meet a deadline, that they are able to do something that has been asked of them, that they will give positive feedback on a suggestion or idea, that they don't need any help—this expectation is so deep in Indian culture, so automatic and instinctive, that it is sufficient for an Indian merely to *refrain* from saying something positive for another Indian to actually hear something negative. It is not necessary, in other words, to actually *say* something that is not pleasing but merely to stop short of saying anything pleasing. This is what is meant by communicating through what is not said (also known as high-context communication), and Indians are very good at it.

Consider the following exchange:

BRIGITTE: I was wondering, Sumitra, if your team can come in on
    Saturday?
SUMITRA: Saturday?
BRIGITTE: Yes. Just for a couple of hours.
SUMITRA: I see.
BRIGITTE: Just to finish up that application test.
SUMITRA: Right.
BRIGITTE: I think Ram's team is coming in also, so it should go
    pretty fast.
SUMITRA: Yes. They work quite fast.
BRIGITTE: So what do you think, Sumitra?

SUMITRA: Let me ask my team and get back to you.
BRIGITTE: No problem.

From the Indian perspective, what stands out quite clearly in this exchange is that Sumitra has been given several opportunities to say that she will come in on Saturday, and she does not. Since Indians assume Sumitra would say "yes" to this request if there was any way she could, thereby giving Brigitte the answer she wants, the fact that Sumitra cannot bring herself to say "yes" is in fact a clear "no." Westerners, who rely mainly on words for their messages, would reach exactly the opposite conclusion: since Sumitra does not actually say anywhere that she can't come in, then she must be coming in (after she checks with her team).

Implying and Suggesting

The other way Indians have of delivering difficult messages, of saying things other people may not want to hear, is through indirection, through *not quite* saying what they really mean. Indians are so attuned to nuance, to reading between the lines, that when other people merely suggest or imply something, the real message comes through loud and clear—to other Indians, that is, although not usually to Westerners.

Indians are so attuned to nuance, to reading between the lines, that when other people merely suggest or imply something, the real message comes through loud and clear.

Let's look at another example.

JOANN: How's everything going, Kartik?
KARTIK: Fine, fine.
JOANN: Are we still on schedule?
KARTIK: Oh yes. We're working extra hard on this.
JOANN: Great. My people are anxious to see the new application.

KARTIK: I'm sure. When are they expecting to see it?

JOANN: By the end of the week, like we agreed.

KARTIK: I see. It turned out to be quite a big job, didn't it?

JOANN: That's for sure. Thanks for all your help, Kartik.

If you can see them, there are several hints in this exchange that Kartik is not on schedule, hints to Westerners, anyway, but closer to out-right declarations to Indians. "We're working extra hard on this" is one. "It turned out to be quite a big job" is another. "When are they expecting to see it?" is yet another (in the sense that since Kartik clearly knows the schedule, then he also knows when Joann's people "are expecting to see" the new application, meaning that this statement is not really a question but a subtle way of saying he's falling behind).

These two principles—communicating by what is not said and by what is only implied—pervade Indian-style communication and show up in numerous techniques Indians regularly use in the workplace. We will examine these techniques in detail in the next chapter.

Young Indians

Before we give a brief overview of Western-style communication, we should probably make a few observations about the younger generation of Indians, a demographic that many Westerners assume to be less traditional, hence more like them, than older Indians. It's true that today's young Indian urban professionals, who are the most likely to be working with Westerners in offshore ventures, are just as likely to have grown up in a nuclear family as in an extended one. And it is, accordingly, tempting to conclude that they are not as collectivist and therefore not as typically Indian in their communication as previous generations.

This is no doubt true to a certain extent, but there are a few caveats that make it less true than Westerners naturally assume. For one, even the nuclear family in India often includes one or more decidedly non-nuclear members, typically an aged parent, grandparent, aunt, or uncle. In urban areas, cousins, nieces, or nephews from the countryside or from other cities often live temporarily in the household while going to school, look-ing for work, or putting together enough money to rent a flat, build a house, or get married. "I cannot remember a time, growing up in India," Shashi Tharoor writes, "when there wasn't a young man from either of my parents villages in Kerala—sometimes not even a close relation—living in our flat while my father arranged for him to have some profes-sional training and get him a job" (1997, 289). And Indian women often live in the household of their husband's family, where they are subject to the influence of their in-laws, especially their mother-in-law. So even the most nuclear of Indian nuclear families often has a decidedly extended feel to it.

We must also remember that even if today's urban professional does not go home to a traditional extended family household—or for that matter may not even have *grown up* in one—his or her parents, teachers, and other elders probably did, and they have therefore passed on to the younger generation of Indians the cultural values and mindset of that kind of collectivist upbringing. While it is probably true, then, that today's Indians are not as collectivist as their parents, they are still more collectivist than they are individualist—and far more collectivist than most Westerners they will ever meet. Richard Lannoy has observed that, "In India, outside a numerically small class, individualism in the Western sense does not exist" (1971, 417).

Communication West: Standing on Your Own Two Feet

As with India, Western-style communication also has its origins in cul-tural values and assumptions, especially the concept of personal identity where, as it happens, Indians and Westerners could scarcely be more dif-ferent. In the same way that Indians are family- and group-oriented, Westerners tend to be individual- and self-oriented. Westerners come from and live in families, too, of course, and must learn to how to get along with others and function in groups, but in most Western cultures there is a second, parallel societal emphasis on the simultaneous develop-ment of the individual.

In the West, the central function of the family is to prepare its members to be able to live on their own, whereas in India the central function of the family is to guarantee that no one ever *has* to live on his or her own (which would be unthinkable and, in many cases, a practical impossibility). Families in the West guide and encourage their members to become independent and self-reliant, to assume responsibility for and increasingly to look after themselves. Individuals are raised to be able "to stand on their own two feet" or "become their own person," as two common expressions have it.

In "Western culture," Kedar Dwivedi has observed,

> independence is viewed as the cherished ideal and dependence . . . is seen as a stigma. The parents are therefore often at pains to make their children independent as soon as possible . . . Children are expected to have their own voices, preferably different from that of their parents. For adolescents, leaving home is considered to be a very important developmental task.
>
> In contrast the Eastern cultures place more emphasis on "dependability." The parents are usually at pains to ensure that their children grow up in an atmosphere where parents are a model of dependability. Such a goal leads to . . . indulgence, immediate gratification of physical and emotional needs, and a rather prolonged babyhood. From the Western point of view this could be seen as a culture of spoilt children. However, it leads to the creation of very strong bonds and provides an inner sense of security and strength. (2002, 47, 48)

Speaking of Americans, this writer has noted elsewhere that they don't like to depend on other people. They don't like to owe them, need them, or be beholden to them. They are generally quite wary of entanglements, of being encumbered, of anything that limits their ability to be true to themselves. In a word, they want to be free—and freedom in the United States boils down to not having to worry about what other people think or what they will say; it means having to answer to no one but yourself. If that sounds like a prescription for loneliness, which it does to many people, Americans would shrug their shoulders and say it's simply the price you have to pay to be independent.

Americans and northern Europeans are not taught to neglect family, of course, but rather to simultaneously develop their own personal, individual identity and autonomy. Whereas an Indian's identity is subsumed within and expressed via the group—indeed, for many Indians it is indistinguishable from that of the group—a Westerner's identity is split. There is, in fact, a great deal of tension in the West between the two halves, between fulfilling the responsibilities to one's family and society at large and the responsibilities to one's self.

Americans are no doubt pre-eminent in the self-reliance sweepstakes, but if northern European cultures do not emphasize personal freedom and independence quite as much, they are still considerably more self- than they are group-oriented, still closer to Americans, in other words, however far apart they may actually be, than they are to Indians.

Individualists

In what is still the best-known and most extensive study of culture in the workplace, the Dutch sociologist Geert Hofstede surveyed people in 66 countries on their attitudes toward certain topics, including this notion of personal identity. Based on participant responses to a number of survey questions, Hofstede ranked countries as "individualist" or "collectivist" according to the following definitions:

> *Individualism* pertains to societies in which the ties between individuals are loose; everyone is expected to look after himself or herself and his or her immediate family.

> *Collectivism* pertains to societies in which people from birth onward are integrated into strong, cohesive groups, which throughout people's lifetimes continue to protect them in exchange for unquestioning loyalty. (1988, 51)

Here are the survey results for India, the United States, the Anglophone countries, and the northern European countries. The higher the number, the more individualist the country; the lower, the more collectivist. The range is from the highest of 91 (USA) to the lowest of 6 (Guatemala), with a mean of 42.

India 48	Finland 63
USA 91	Germany 67
Great Britain 89	Netherlands 80
Canada 80	Norway 69
Australia 90	Sweden 71
New Zealand 79	Switzerland 68
Denmark 74	

Source: Hofstede, 1991, p. 53

Hofstede noted that a difference of as little as 10 points between any two countries would likely show up as significant differences in workplace attitudes and behaviors. All the Western countries on our list are on the other side of the mean from India; all but two (Finland and Germany) are separated from India by more than 20 points; and the United States and most of the Anglophone countries are separated from India by 30 points or more (and by 43 and 41 points, respectively, for the United States and Great Britain).

By and large, Westerners have not been raised in extended families and do not grow up learning how to maneuver and manipulate within an extensive family hierarchy. Individual survival and well-being do not depend as much on the sufferance and goodwill of others and, therefore, on being so closely attuned and responsive to the feelings, moods, and wishes of others. Whatever cultural conditioning Westerners get in learning how to survive inside a group, it is minimal compared with what Indians experience. Moreover, where the survival of the group is not paramount, considerations such as group harmony and the related necessity for saving face do not loom large. Indeed, for all intents and purposes, the notion of saving face does not operate in the West, at least not as it is generally understood in Asia.

Impact on Communication Style

If the overriding goal of Indian-style communication is to preserve and strengthen personal relationships, the overriding goal in the West is to exchange information.

If the overriding goal of Indian-style communication is to preserve and strengthen personal relationships, the overriding goal in Western-style communication is to exchange information. What the other person does or does not want to hear is largely irrelevant to Westerners since they don't depend on the goodwill of others for their own well-being. Hence, Westerners are free to say what they're thinking. Indeed, when one Westerner talks to another that is precisely the goal: to convey what is in the mind of the speaker—his or her ideas, opinions, knowledge, wishes—to the mind of the listener. Accordingly, Westerners are taught to "say what you mean" and to "mean what you say," and generally they adhere to this advice whenever possible. "The value orientation of individualism," two cultural analysts have noted, "propels North Americans to speak their minds freely through direct verbal expression. Individualistic values foster the norms of honesty and openness. Honesty and openness are achieved through the use of precise, straightforward language" (Gudykunst and Ting-Toomey 1988, 102).

But even Westerners know that you can't always say what you're thinking or mean everything you say. Westerners are not completely oblivious to the feelings of others, after all, and are, in fact, quite capable of being diplomatic and tactful when the occasion calls for it. But that's just the point: the occasion calls for it far less often in the West than in India.

Needless to say, there isn't much room in such a scheme for hearing what people *don't* say or what they don't *quite* say, for reading between the lines, or for otherwise sensing or somehow intuiting the message. For Westerners the words *are* the message, and messages that come in other forms usually don't get delivered.

Clearly, then, Indians and Westerners are on something of a collision course when it comes to communication style; even as Westerners are busy trying to "speak their mind," Indians are busy trying to read and speak the *other person's* mind. In the next chapter, we will examine the most common problems caused by this cultural mismatch and offer advice on how to minimize the damage.

But before we go: Some readers may still be scratching their heads over the Bill-Deepak story at the beginning of this chapter. What *was* Deepak trying to tell Bill? It's really not all that obscure once one starts reading between the lines: Deepak has no doubt been planning his wedding for some time; so, to begin with, one has to wonder why he has picked this particular day to inform Bill about it, the same day, it should be noted, Bill announces that the schedule for the new application is being moved forward. Coincidence? Probably not. One also has to wonder why Deepak insists on bringing the wedding up at each weekly update, since Bill told him at the outset that he and his wife will not be attending. Finally, one has to wonder why the date on the announcements was wrong. Could it be the date had to be changed because Deepak had to postpone the wedding? Could it be, in short, that every time Deepak meets with Bill he is politely "asking" him for more time to complete the application so he doesn't have to further delay his wedding? And if that's true (which it was), and if it is also true that Deepak assumes Bill has understood all this (which he did), then is it any wonder Deepak concludes that Bill is a pretty rigid guy?

Yes, No, and Other Problems

*Every country has its own way of saying things. The important
point is that which lies behind people's words.*

Freya Stark
The Journey's Echo

In the last chapter we looked at the big picture, the cultural origins of the
Indian and Western styles of communication. In this chapter we look at
the details, at what actually happens in the workplace when people with
such different styles try to talk to each other.

The Indian "Yes"

A good place to start our discussion is with one of the earliest and most
common problems Westerners typically encounter when they begin
working with Indians: the word "yes." "Yes" is the indispensable word in
Indian culture, as it is in all collectivist cultures where preserving harmony and maintaining good interpersonal relations are two of the greatest goods. Simply stated, how can you ever disappoint, upset, embarrass,
or offend other people, especially those above you in the hierarchy, if you
always respond with "yes," regardless (one hastens to add) of what you
really think or of what the truth might be? "India has a hierarchical society," Paul Davies observes, "[and] hierarchies depend on not giving
offense. If you can't give offense up or down the hierarchy, you can't possibly say no to anything. 'Yes' therefore has to stand for all sorts of words

and can mean anything" (Davies 2004, 130). Indian culture would be unthinkable—and completely unworkable—without "yes." The fact that it doesn't mean anything is beside the point.

That's probably too strong. Of course "yes" means something; it means several things, in fact, but none of them, unfortunately, are what Westerners mean by "yes." For Americans and Europeans "yes" is a positive answer to a question or inquiry, as in I understand, I agree, I accept, I approve. When Westerners say "yes," it is usually an answer to a question, and when they *hear* "yes," they assume it's the answer to their question.

This is where the trouble starts, because for Indians the word "yes" *by itself* is really the equivalent of the Western "Uh huh." It only means I'm listening, I'm taking in what you're saying, I'm hearing you, I'm enjoying the sound of your voice. In other words, it's not a positive answer but merely a polite response, a routine acknowledgement. Indeed, just as the Western "uh huh" can be followed by any kind of answer—a positive answer, a negative answer, or something in between—the same is true for the Indian "yes." And just as Westerners know not to take "uh huh" for an answer and wait to hear what the person says next, they should likewise not take the Indian "yes" for an answer and wait to hear what the Indian says next.

The origin of the "yes" problem, incidentally, probably has something to do with the Hindi word *Accha*, which is almost the exact equivalent of "uh huh" but which Indians mistakenly think can be translated as "yes." The bottom line is when Indians say "yes," they're actually thinking *Accha*—I hear you. They do not consider it an answer to a question—and they assume Westerners don't, either.

We should mention that we're using the word "yes" here merely as one example of a whole category of expressions Indians use to communicate "I hear you" and nothing else. Some of the other expressions, used instead of or along with "yes," are: sure, fine, OK, I see, and no problem. When used as the initial response to something a Westerner says, each of these words should be seen for what it is: pure politeness and nothing more.

When used as the initial response to something a Westerner says,
[the word "yes"] should be seen for what it is: pure politeness
and nothing more.

So how does one know, the reader may be wondering, when you're
getting a real "yes" and when you're just getting "I hear you?" That's easy;
since "yes" merely means "uh huh," just disregard the "yes" (in the same
way you would disregard "uh huh") and listen to what the Indian says
next. If that contains the usual indicators of a positive response, which are
the same for Indians as for Americans, then it *is* a positive response. If it
does not contain such indicators, then beware (see below).

The Indian "Yes" Head Gesture

We should briefly note the common problem Westerners have with the
Indian head gesture for "yes." For many Indians, especially in the southern half of the country, this gesture is a kind of head wobble or bobbing
motion, tilting but not turning the head to one side and then tilting it to
the other, that looks very much like the way Westerners shake their head
to indicate "no." If one looks closely, the difference between the two gestures is apparent, but if a person is not looking closely, it's very easy to
confuse the Indian head wobble with the Western "no" and get the wrong
idea. For the record, the Indian and the Western head gesture for "no" are
the same: the unilateral head sweep, a distinctive turning of the head
to one side, turning it back to face forward, and then turning it to the
other side.

The head tilt is not the "yes" gesture for all Indians, of course, and
many will, in fact, vigorously deny that people in India make this gesture.
Other Indians, when asked about the gesture, will laugh uproariously and
own up to it. (An Indian reader once e-mailed me about a "great mistake"
I had made in an earlier book where I described this gesture, and he asked
that the reference be removed in subsequent printings because "no one in
India ever does this.")

The Indian "No"

Believe it or not, the Indian "no" causes infinitely more communication problems for Westerners than the Indian "yes." Once you know that 'yes' just means "uh huh," the "yes" problem usually goes away. The "no" problem, alas, is much more complicated and intractable.

In group-oriented Indian culture, having to tell other people what they *don't* want to hear—in a word, having to tell them "no"—poses a conspicuous problem.

Indians are culturally conditioned not to cause offense and to tell other people what they want to hear, especially superiors and one's elders. What safer way to guarantee harmony and save face, after all, than never to disagree, never to confront? Not surprisingly, then, in the hierarchical, group-oriented Indian culture, having to tell other people what they *don't* want to hear—in a word, having to tell them "no" in any of its various forms—poses a conspicuous problem. "Indians will have extreme difficulty using the word 'no,'" Paul Davies has written, "even when they might mean it. I'm not sure an Indian *can* even mean 'no' without some threat to his or her sleeping patterns" (italics added) (Davies, 129). An American told me a story of a young Indian man at a meeting who was apparently so shocked at something another participant asked him that he immediately responded with a very strong "no" and was so embarrassed that he apologized for the rest of the meeting and sent a follow-up e-mail to the "offended" party (who didn't see what the fuss was all about).

Actually, Indians have solved the "no" problem quite neatly: they just never say "no." That is, they never resort to the word "no" or to any other blatantly negative formulation. Indians manage to communicate all the negative messages the rest of us do using words like "no" or "not"— disagreeing, refusing, saying something is not possible, expressing dislike, turning someone down, and generally delivering bad news—they're just less obvious and much more discreet about it (to Westerners, that is).

For people who need to hear the word "no" in order to grasp that they've gotten a negative response, a category that would include most Americans and Europeans, the fact that Indians almost never use this word is the source of a great deal of serious confusion.

We'll examine that confusion more closely in a moment, but first we should probably mention one circumstance under which Indians actually do use the word "no," quite readily, in fact, and that is when a superior is talking to a subordinate. The highly hierarchical nature of Indian society permits superiors to be very blunt, almost rude, to their underlings, which, because it is entirely expected, does not actually disturb the harmony of the group. So when we say Indians never use the word "no," we really mean that subordinates, underlings, younger people, and anyone else deemed as being in a lesser role doesn't use the word "no" with those people they regard as being of a superior rank or station. In this context, we would point out that Indian vendors working for an American or European company would consider themselves in a subordinate position in this relationship and typically would not be comfortable saying "no" to the Western client.

The Absence of "Yes"

So how do Indians say "no" then? The short answer is: by not saying "yes." By and large the Indian "no" is not a negative statement, but rather the conspicuous absence of a positive statement *in a context where "yes" is clearly desired and/or expected.* As noted earlier, "Yes" in its various forms—yes, fine, sure, OK, no problem—is so culturally mandated and so deeply anticipated in Indian culture that it is enough for one Indian simply *not to say* "yes" for another Indian to understand "no." Nothing negative has actually been said, but much more important something positive has very obviously *not* been said. And that is in fact the message.

This isn't logical to many Americans and northern Europeans, of course, who have trouble understanding how something that has not been said can be a message, to say nothing of how it can be *obvious.* But logic, alas, is one of the earliest casualties when West meets East.

This will all be clearer if we look at some examples. Consider the following exchange between Marian and her Indian colleague Kumar.

KUMAR: Marian! How are you?
MARIAN: I'm fine, thanks. I was wondering, Kumar, what you would
    think if we decided to move up the date for the systems test?
KUMAR: Move it up?
MARIAN: Just by a week, at the most.
KUMAR: I see. Do you think it's possible?
MARIAN: Should be. But what do *you* think?
KUMAR: Me? I guess you don't see any problems?
MARIAN: Not really. My people can be ready at this end if your
    people can be up to speed by then.
KUMAR: I see.

It's clear from the beginning of this exchange that Marian would like to move up the date for the systems test if possible. Why else would she raise the subject? This is what we meant in the previous paragraph when we talked about "a context where 'yes' is clearly desired." This is the point where Kumar would say "yes" if he could, and the fact that he does not, even when given several more opportunities, is very meaningful in Indian culture—and what it means is "It's not possible." But it doesn't mean "not possible" to Marian, of course, who needs to get an actual negative answer—and not simply *not get* a positive one—to understand that Kumar is turning her down.

Here's another example:

BILL: We need to schedule our tour of your facility.
ANU: Of course.
BILL: How about next Tuesday morning?
ANU: Tuesday?
BILL: Yes, would 10:30 be OK?
ANU: 10:30? Is it good for you?
BILL: Yes, it's fine.

Here again it seems obvious Bill would like to schedule a tour for next Tuesday, and Anu would certainly agree to this if there was any way she could. When Bill proposes "next Tuesday morning," then, and Anu merely repeats the suggestion ("Tuesday?") instead of agreeing to it, then she is in fact saying that Tuesday is not convenient. Bill doesn't pick up on this, of course, and moves ahead to set the time; Anu again fails to agree ("Is it good for you?"); and once again Bill doesn't understand. Bill walks away assuming Tuesday is fine, and Anu leaves thinking Bill will eventually propose a new time for the tour.

Unintended Consequences

This is the moment where most communication problems between Indians and Westerners begin: the point where the Indian says "no," or, more accurately, where the Indian *communicates* "no" (since the Indian never actually uses the word), the Westerner does not hear "no," the Indian believes the Westerner has understood, and the Westerner likewise believes he or she has understood. Marian, for example, may go ahead and move up the date for the systems test because she thinks Kumar has not objected, and Bill may go ahead and schedule the tour for Tuesday because Anu never said it wouldn't suit her. When Marian later discovers Kumar is not ready for the systems test on the new date and when Bill can't find Anu on Tuesday, Marian will be upset with Kumar (for misleading her into thinking the new date was fine), and Bill will be irritated with Anu (who agreed to be available on Tuesday when clearly she was not). Kumar and Anu, meanwhile, will be quite surprised when these two Westerners get upset with them because both Indians genuinely believe they have been quite clear that they cannot do what has been asked of them.

The real problem with such incidents, the reason both parties need to avoid or at least try to minimize them, is not so much the actual misunderstanding that takes place here but the unfortunate consequences it leads to. When Indians and Westerners both mistakenly believe communication has been successful, as in these two examples, this dynamic immediately sets up inaccurate expectations that can only result down the road in surprise, at best, but more often in disappointment, frustration, and mutual mistrust.

When Indians and Westerners both mistakenly believe there has been successful communication, this can only result down the road in surprise, frustration, and mutual mistrust.

Neither side wants this to happen, of course, and in a moment we will describe how these cultural incidents can be avoided. But first it is important to make the point that these incidents are in fact legitimate, honest misunderstandings, with neither party (or both parties equally) at fault. If we examine the scenarios objectively, it cannot be said that one party is somehow more responsible for what happened here than the other. The Indians did not realize the Westerners had misunderstood them (or they would have said something), and the Westerners honestly believed they had understood the Indians (or they would have asked questions). In other words, the Indians did not intend to mislead the Westerners, and, for their part, the Westerners weren't trying to misread the Indians.

There has still been a misunderstanding, with serious and unfortunate consequences, but it helps both parties if they can understand that what happened was completely unintentional. If Marian and Bill believed they had been deliberately misled, they would be justifiably upset, and likewise if Kumar and Anu thought the Westerners had deliberately misinterpreted them. But when each side understands that the mistakes were quite innocent, that neither the Indians nor the Westerners intended or were aware of what was happening—indeed, that they would be appalled to realize what was happening—then everyone can calm down. We still have a problem—we don't want these things to happen and we need to prevent them as much as possible—but at least now we realize that no one was acting in bad faith. While this doesn't make the issue go away, it does take the sting out of the situation, and that goes a long way toward restoring good working relations.

Even legitimate problems are still problems, of course, and in need of a solution. So let's continue our analysis of Indian communication style. Earlier we were looking at the Indian "no," and we had established that Indians never actually say "no"; they just refrain from saying "yes," and that means "no" to other Indians. Indians actually have a number of ways of refraining from saying "yes," each of which we will now describe in more detail.

The "No-Response" Response

One of the most common ways Indians communicate "no" is not to say anything in response to an inquiry. Suppose you send an e-mail to an Indian colleague suggesting a solution to a coding problem, and the Indian, who is always very good about answering his e-mails, does not respond. There's a good chance this lack of a response is, in fact, his response—and it's not a positive one. Remember: if there's any way the Indian could respond positively to your suggestion and tell you what you want to hear, he would do so immediately, heartily commending you on your most excellent logic. If he doesn't respond, therefore, it's probably because your logic, sadly, is not especially excellent. Nothing has actually been said, of course, and that's precisely the point: praise has been conspicuously withheld. And everybody knows what *that* means.

Avoiding the Question or Changing the Subject

Another way to get around saying "no" is to simply dodge or avoid any question that would have to be answered in the negative, which is often accomplished simply by changing the subject.

KARL: Ashok, how's the data analysis going?
ASHOK: Not too bad.
KARL: Will it be ready for the meeting?
ASHOK: The meeting? Right. When is that scheduled for again?
KARL: Friday. Your guys will be ready, right?

ASHOK: Actually I wanted to ask you about the meeting. Who's
  going to be there exactly?
KARL: Well, my team, Sharon's team, and probably Eric's people.
ASHOK: I see. Should be very interesting.

In this exchange, Ashok has twice steered the conversation away from
Karl's inquiry about whether the data analysis is going to be ready in time
for the upcoming meeting. The Indian assumes Karl will understand
what this means—that he (Ashok) doesn't want to answer this particular
question—and furthermore that Karl will also understand the reason:
that the analysis will not be ready in time. After all, why would Ashok not
want to answer the question if the analysis was going to be ready? Indeed,
Ashok expects that at any moment Karl will ask him if he needs more
time to complete the analysis (for this is what another Indian would do at
this juncture). The point here is that when Indians avoid your question,
it's because there's something wrong with your question, and what's
wrong with it is that it would require a negative answer.

The Postponed Answer

A related technique here is to postpone or put off the answer to a
question or request, using replies such as these:

"Let me ask my team."
"I'll get back to you on that."
"Let me look into it."
"Can I call you later?"
"Can we talk about this another time?"
"I'll make some inquiries."
"Let me follow up on that."

Once again, the principle here is that you're not really getting a
response to your inquiry, which can only mean one of two things: either
the Indian is not able to answer your question at this time, or he is not

willing to answer. If the person is not willing, then we are back in "no" territory, for why would someone be unwilling to answer a question in the affirmative? If you receive replies like the above, then, you can either take them as a "no" or wait a short while (usually no more than a day) to see if the Indian actually does bring the matter up again. If the matter is not brought up again, then that's your answer. Westerners typically follow up in such cases, assuming the Indian has forgotten, at which point Westerners will need to be alert to all the other varieties of "no."

Repeating the Question

Another way to not answer a question (thereby giving a negative answer) is to simply repeat the question, in effect sending it back to the questioner. This is what Kumar does in his first exchange with Marian when he responds, "Move it up?" to her question about whether it's possible to change the date for the systems test. Clearly, if Kumar thought it were possible, he would say so at this point. When he tries to avoid the question, therefore, he's indicating that moving the date forward is not possible.

Anu does the same thing twice in her exchange with Bill. When he asks her if Tuesday would be OK for the tour, she simply repeats "Tuesday?" If Tuesday were possible, why would she repeat the question and not simply say "yes"? When Bill then asks if 10:30 would be OK, Anu again repeats the question. Once again, what the Westerner needs to understand is that Indians would not repeat questions they were quite comfortable answering. So if the Indian is not comfortable, one has to ask oneself why, and surely the reason would *never* be that the Indian is going to have to answer "yes."

Turning the Question on the Speaker

Kumar and Anu both use another common technique of responding in the negative: they ask the two Westerners what they think of their own suggestions. When Marian asks Kumar if he thinks it's possible to move up the date for the systems test, Kumar turns the question on her: "I see. Do you think it's possible?" When Marian persists and asks Kumar point blank what he thinks, he again turns the question on her: "I guess you don't see any problems?" Similarly, when Bill asks Anu if 10:30 on Tuesday is a good time for the tour, she responds by asking him: "Is that good for you?" When Indians turn your questions back on you, when they won't answer your question, that *is* your answer.

Some of the most common examples of questions that are usually negative replies include any form of the following:

"Does that work for you?"
"Is that good for you?"
"Do you think that's possible?"
"Is that what you would like?"
"I'm not sure. What do you think?"

Hesitation

Another indication of "no" from Indians is any kind of obvious hesitation in response to a question or request. Coming from people who instinctively and automatically agree whenever possible, the slightest hesitation is a not-so-subtle sign of trouble. This hesitation can take several forms: one is a period of silence preceding the Indian's response; another is body language that indicates how uncomfortable the Indian is with the question or request, such as a nervous laugh, wrinkling of the brow, a quick intake of breath; another is tone of voice indicating how painful the question is; and another is a noncommittal response, such as the very common "I see" (which Kumar says twice to Marian). What the Westerner must remember here is that when Indians can't immediately commit, when they are obviously weighing their answer, it's not a good sign (and probably *is* their answer).

The Qualified or Conditional "Yes"

In addition to avoiding questions that would require a negative answer, another way Indians express "no" is with a qualified or conditional "yes."

Whenever you get a positive response—sure, fine, yes, OK, great—followed by one of the common qualified responses listed below, you should follow up to see what the Indian means, or simply accept the answer as an outright "no," which is most likely what is intended:

"That should be OK/possible."
"That might be OK/possible."
"That shouldn't be a problem."
"We'll do our very best."
"Perhaps."
"Maybe."
"Possibly."
"Probably."
"Good chance."
"Good possibility."
"I think so."
"We can try."

What is most significant in any exchange like this is the fact that the Indian has not quite managed to respond with an unequivocal "yes," for which there is no doubt a very good reason. What usually happens in these exchanges is that the Indian, who is very attuned to nuance, expects the Westerner to hear the qualifier and discount the "yes," whereas in fact the Westerner, generally less conditioned to pay attention to nuance, hears the "yes" and discounts the qualifier.

For Indians, qualifiers are usually not something between "yes" and "no": they are much closer to "no."

The other cultural difference here is the meaning of qualifiers in India and in the West. In the West, qualifiers are something between "yes" and "no," but they are generally closer to "yes." For Indians, on the other hand, qualifiers are usually not something *between* "yes" and "no": they are much closer to "no." You can always probe with a follow-up inquiry if you're not sure what the Indian is telling you, but if the Indian then becomes uncomfortable or uses any of the other techniques described in this section, then the qualified "yes" you just got was indeed a "no."

Combined Forms

Needless to say, Indians often combine one or more of these forms of "no" in the same exchange, depending on the situation. Here's an example of no less than five in one short conversation (a slightly altered version of the exchange between Sumitra and Brigitte in chapter 2). See if you can find them.

> BRIGITTE: I was wondering, Sumitra, if your team can come in on
>   Saturday?
> SUMITRA: Saturday?
> BRIGITTE: Yes. Just for a couple of hours.
> SUMITRA: I see.
> BRIGITTE: Just to finish up that application test.
> SUMITRA: Right.
> BRIGITTE: I think Ram's team is coming in also, so it should go
>   pretty fast.
> SUMITRA: Yes. They work quite fast.
> BRIGITTE: So what do you think, Sumitra?
> SUMITRA: That's probably OK.
> BRIGITTE: That's great.
> SUMITRA: Let me ask my team and get back to you.
> BRIGITTE: No problem.

Brigitte has been told five times that Sumitra is not available on Saturday, but there's every indication that she's still expecting the Indian to come in. On Monday, therefore, Brigitte is legitimately going to be very annoyed with Sumitra for "misleading" her, and Sumitra is legitimately going to be very surprised (and maybe hurt) since she told Brigitte several times she could not come in on Saturday. As we noted before, these are legitimate, innocent misunderstandings—neither party expects nor desires the decidedly unfortunate outcome—but that doesn't change the result.

Bad News

Figuring out the Indian "yes" and the Indian "no" are certainly the two biggest communication challenges Americans and Europeans face and the source of more misunderstandings than any other cultural difference. But there are at least two other common challenges that come under the communication umbrella and deserve special attention: the way Indians deliver bad news and the way they give negative feedback. As the reader can well imagine, these are very delicate topics, fraught with implications for harmony and face and therefore requiring Indians to tread very carefully. And whenever Indians tread carefully, as we have seen throughout this chapter, Westerners are unable to follow.

Bad news is never something people want to hear, which makes delivering it, especially to clients, customers, or to one's boss, quite painful for Indians. A lot of bad news gets delivered in the form of a negative response to an inquiry or a request, and we have already described in detail the many forms negative answers can take with Indians. But sometimes Indians initiate the bad news, and Westerners have to listen closely to catch it.

Behind Schedule

Probably the most common and most frustrating example for Westerners is when Indians have to admit that they are not on schedule, need more time, or are going to miss a deadline. Admitting these things is very uncomfortable in Indian culture; so as is the case with all difficult or delicate topics, Indians have worked out certain prescribed formulas for delivering this news without actually saying the dreaded words. The problem with these formulas is that Westerners do not understand them, with the usual result that Indians assume they have communicated the bad news when in fact they have not. This is especially unfortunate in the case of a missed deadline because by the time Westerners discover the Indians are in fact late and by the time Indians realize Westerners thought they were on time—a moment that is usually very close to or even the same as the deadline —it's too late to do anything except, perhaps, engage in mutual recriminations!

So what are these formulas Indians use to announce they going to miss a deadline? They are different in different situations, of course, but it's possible to list a few common conversational gambits that are very often stand-ins for and early warnings of "We're getting behind." They include:

Repeatedly bringing up the subject of the schedule or deadline (to prompt you to ask if they need more time).
Mentioning that the schedule is inconvenient or ambitious.
Asking if the deadline is still good for you.
Asking if all parts of the work need to be done by the deadline or if certain parts could be done later.
Talking about how busy they have become.
Mentioning that part of the project is taking longer than expected.
Mentioning that some parts of the project *are* on schedule.
Asking if members of another team are busy or observing that they don't appear to be very busy.
Mentioning how late people are working each day or how much overtime people are putting in.
Mentioning that some people are coming in on the weekends.
Pointing out how another team was recently given more time to finish their project.

The point is that while these seemingly innocuous comments would in fact raise alarms among fellow Indians, who would respond by asking if the schedule needed to be adjusted, Westerners would usually overlook them. And with good reason; most of these remarks make no direct reference to the actual subject, and those that *do* mention the schedule stay well away from any reference to being late or needing more time. In the first instance, Westerners will not even realize that the schedule is the topic of discussion, and in the second they would not normally interpret the remarks as cries for help.

That's Not Possible

Another type of bad news that is difficult for Indians to deliver is to say that something is not possible, that they are not able or available (for whatever reason) to do something other people have asked of them. The strong desire to please, and beyond that to be responsive and helpful to the client, the boss, or one's elders, makes it hard for Indians to refuse a request.

Indeed, Indians are so aware of how awkward it is for someone to have to refuse a request that they have devised a strategy for making sure that the situation almost never arises. When Indians have a request to make and they're not sure the other person can agree to it—when it's possible, in other words, that the other person might have to say "no"—Indians are careful to never actually make the request. What they do instead is make it quite clear through comments and observations that they could use some help if the other person was so inclined, and then wait to see how the other person responds. If the Indian is free and willing to help, she will offer assistance. If the Indian is not free and willing, she will simply say nothing. In this way the Indian is never put in the awkward position of having to turn down the "request" because, in fact, no request was ever made.

But awkward requests do sometimes come about, even among Indians—and routinely with Westerners—so Indians have worked out ways to turn down such requests and still preserve harmony. These approaches involve the usual polite circumlocution (from the Western point of view) and avoid any direct refusal. We have already examined several of these formulas when we described the various Indian ways of saying "no," but there are a few other responses Westerners should also be aware of (all preceded, of course, with some form of "yes").

Answering with any kind of qualifier: "That might be possible." "We can probably do that." "We'll try our best."

Postponing the answer: "Let me ask my team." "Can I get back to you on that?" "I'll check my calendar."

Not answering or responding with a question: "Do you think that's possible?" "Is that what you'd like?" "Would you like us to be available?"

Making references to how busy they are.

Agreeing to the request and then bringing it up or asking about it again later in the conversation or in a subsequent e-mail.

Once again, no words are used that constitute an outright refusal, but much more important (for Indians) neither were any words used which constitute clear agreement. Westerners listen for the former, of course, and assume their request has been agreed to; Indians expect Westerners to listen for the latter and realize they've been turned down.

Asking for Help

Another awkward situation for Indians is to have to ask for help, to admit that they don't know how to do something, for example, or that they don't have the resources or time to do something that has been asked of them, especially if this is something they have previously said they could do. This is a potentially embarrassing situation in most cultures, of course, not just in India, but it is especially acute in face-saving cultures.

The Indian way of handling this situation, not surprisingly, is to never actually ask for help but merely to make it clear that help is needed, and then wait for the other party to respond. Common techniques Indians use to ask for help include:

Repeatedly mentioning how busy they are.

Mentioning that something is taking longer than expected.

Implying that a deadline might be missed (hoping you will then ask why).

Mentioning that something was more complicated or more involved than they had originally thought.

Talking about another team that recently needed and received help.

Talking about a time in the past when they received help in a very similar situation.

As usual, the Indian way of handling this delicate situation is never to actually make a request for help in so many words; what Indians typically do instead is to make it very clear they could use some help and then wait to see how the other party responds. In India, the other party will then offer help if he is able or willing to do so or simply say nothing if he is not. Westerners, who won't hear any request for help in such statements, will not realize (1) that Indians are in trouble and need assistance and (2) that by not offering assistance, Indians will assume the Westerners are not able or willing to help them.

Negative Feedback

It happens quite often in the workplace that one party asks a second party what he thinks of an idea, a proposal, or how something has been done. And the second party tells the first party what she thinks. This sounds pretty simple, but as the astute reader will have by now figured out, nothing is ever simple when you're dealing with someone from a different culture. For Indians, positive feedback is automatic and almost instinctive, the very embodiment of the Indian cultural imperative of telling other people what they want to hear. Negative feedback, needless to say, has nothing in common with telling people what they want to hear and for Indians, therefore, is practically akin to torture.

Negative feedback, needless to say, has nothing in common with telling people what they want to hear and for Indians, therefore, is practically akin to torture.

Consider the following exchange:

BILL: So what did you guys think of that suggestion I e-mailed you about last week?

SUNIL: Last week?

BILL: You know, the idea to . . . . ?

SUNIL: Oh, yes. I remember. Yes, we got that one.

BILL: And?

SUNIL: We had some good discussions.

BILL: Great. What did you think?

SUNIL: Deepok actually had another idea.

BILL: Great. I'd like to hear it, but before that, what did you think of my suggestion?

SUNIL: You'd like us to try that, then?

BILL: If you think it would work.

SUNIL: We liked the one part where you said . . . .

BILL: Great.

This exchange, which we will decode in a moment, contains five of the most common methods Indians use to give negative feedback. These are not methods Americans and most Europeans use, however, nor do they understand these methods when they are on the receiving end of them. Indians assume Westerners do understand these formulas, of course, and we thus again have in place all the essential ingredients for a full-blown cultural misunderstanding.

The whole matter of negative feedback puts us back into the "no" territory explored earlier in this chapter, and the techniques Indians use to express this kind of feedback, such as disapproval or criticism, have much in common with their approaches to saying "no." Indeed, the operative concept is almost identical: just as Indians communicate "no" by conspicuously not saying "yes," negative feedback is essentially the absence of positive feedback in circumstances where Indians have been asked to give their opinion. In other words, if an Indian does not say something positive in a situation where he or she has been asked for feedback, then this conspicuous omission is in all likelihood negative feedback. Indians never actually *say* anything negative in these circumstances, much like they never actually say the word "no"; they just refrain from saying anything positive.

Negative feedback is in some ways even more difficult for Indians than saying "no." It's one thing to disappoint or even annoy other people, but it's quite another to criticize them, thereby causing a possible loss of face. If Indians have to be careful and resort to all manner of circumlocutions just to say "no," imagine the lengths they have to go to dress up negative feedback. Indeed, that's precisely the problem; most Westerners *can't* imagine how Indians do this and usually miss the feedback altogether. Some of the most common forms of Indian-style negative feedback are evident when we closely examine the exchange between Bill and Sunil.

No Response

Though he doesn't know it, Bill has already received Sunil's feedback on his suggestion even before this conversation opens. Bill sent Sunil an e-mail the previous week with a proposal about something the two men are working on, and Sunil never responded. In Indian culture, this *is* Sunil's response, and it is negative. We must remind ourselves again what's going on in an Indian's mind in this situation: Sunil would love nothing more than to be able to heap praise on Bill's wonderful suggestion, thereby preserving and strengthening his and Bill's excellent working relationship and, not incidentally, saving Bill's face (which would be at risk if Sunil criticized Bill's suggestion). Under such strong cultural pressure to say something positive, if Sunil is so bold as not to reply to Bill's e-mail, then it's clear what Sunil thinks. (It's always possible, of course, that Sunil did not get the e-mail or did not have time to respond, but it is made clear in the next sentence that Sunil did get it.)

The problem here, of course, is that for Europeans and Americans, no response is not negative feedback; it's the *absence* of feedback because for Westerners, negative feedback means actually *saying something* negative.

The Repeated Question

Needless to say, Sunil is quite surprised that Bill did not understand his non-response and that Bill has now tracked Sunil down to ask him in person what he thinks of Bill's proposal. This is exactly the kind of face-to-face confrontation Sunil had hoped to avoid by not answering Bill's e-mail. Sunil tries to deflect the confrontation with another technique that we have already examined—the repeated (hence unanswered) question—when he says "Last week?" As noted earlier, when Indians try not to answer a question, it's usually because if they were to answer it would have to be in the negative.

A Very Loud Silence

When this technique doesn't work, an increasingly uncomfortable Sunil moves on to his next version of negative feedback, which we might call the loud silence, when he admits he did receive Bill's e-mail: "Oh, yes. I remember. Yes, we got that one." And then says nothing else during the excruciating silence that follows. This is the point where Indians would immediately add how much they liked Bill's suggestion. The fact that Sunil says nothing during this very pregnant pause is quite significant.

Sunil's next comment—"We had some good discussions"—is effectively more of the same, for this sets up yet another logical place to follow up with positive feedback. Once again, the silence at the end of this observation, the space Sunil leaves conspicuously blank instead of saying what the team thought of Bill's idea, is extremely telling. Alas, it doesn't tell Bill anything because Bill needs messages in the form of words.

Suggesting an Alternative

Sunil's next technique is to comment on Bill's idea by suggesting an alternative. Once again he deliberately sidesteps Bill's direct question ("What did you think?" which is in fact a response) and then mentions that Deepok has another idea. The real message here is not that Deepok has an idea worthy of discussion, although that is important, but that Bill does not. When Indians say nothing about a proposal and offer an alternative instead—in effect, making a counterproposal—this is as much a comment on the original proposal as it is a conversation about the alternative.

Asking Your Opinion

Beginning to exhaust his repertory, Sunil now tries yet another approach by asking Bill what he thinks of his own suggestion: "You'd like us to try that, then?" As noted earlier, this type of question is almost never a question with Indians; it's an observation. Of course Bill would like the Indians to try his suggestion! Why else would he have made it? Sunil knows this too, of course, so when he asks Bill if he wants the Indians to try his idea, this can't really be a question. And it's not. It is, rather, a polite way of saying that Sunil thinks it won't work, polite because it comes in the form of a query rather than in the blunt form of a statement, but the meaning is the same. Notice, too, that Sunil uses the qualifier "try," suggesting pointedly that he has some doubt as to whether this idea will work.

Damning with Faint Praise

Not pointed for Bill, however, thereby forcing Sunil to try yet another technique when he says, "We liked the one part where you said . . . " This technique, sometimes referred to as praising the part to dismiss the whole, allows Indians to say something positive about a suggestion or proposal even as they are dismissing it. The essence of the technique is to admire a detail, a minor, unimportant feature of the proposal ("one part"), and say nothing about the core or centerpiece. The real message— We're not commenting on the essence of your suggestion (and you, of course, know why that is)—is not lost on Indians. It is lost on Bill, however ("Great."), at which point Sunil has run out of techniques.

Bill probably walks away from this exchange assuming there's at least an even chance his suggestion is going to work, especially since Sunil has never criticized the proposal. For his part Sunil, who has made it repeatedly clear that Bill's suggestion is unworkable, walks away assuming Bill knows this, believing Bill wants him to try out the idea anyway (since Bill keeps pushing his idea in the face of Sunil's persistent criticism), and assuming Bill realizes that there's little chance of success. As the curtain falls, we are left again with the familiar scene of Indians and Westerners believing themselves to be moving forward on parallel tracks when in fact they're on a collision course.

To recapitulate, the most common forms of negative feedback Indian-style, just like the forms of saying "no" Indian-style, do not involve the use of negative words; they involve the conspicuous absence of positive words. They do not involve commenting on the topic but studiously avoiding all invitations to comment on the topic (or commenting on another topic). And the meaning is not in what is said but in what is not said. Is it any wonder that a common Western complaint is that "Indians never tell us when they don't like something or when they don't think something will work"? Any wonder either, as it happens, that Indians for their part are quite surprised to hear this?

When Westerners Talk Like Indians

At this point, Western readers may be asking themselves a question: If we are supposed to interpret all these techniques for saying "no," communicating bad news, and giving negative feedback to mean what Indians mean when they say these things, then do Indians think *we* mean these things when we accidentally use these same techniques in *our* speech (accidentally in the sense that Westerners don't usually mean "no" when they talk this way)? In other words, if an American says "I think so" in response to something an Indian asks, will the Indian think the American is actually saying "no?"

The short answer here is: of course. Indians interpret the messages they receive from other people to mean the same thing they would mean if an Indian said those things. But in fact the truth here may be a little more complicated. Certainly some Indians will think a Westerner is saying "no" if he responds with a qualified "yes," for example, or that the Westerner is giving negative feedback by praising only part of a proposal, in particular those Indians who have not had enough contact with Westerners to realize that they don't use these techniques the way Indians do. But Indians who have had some experience with Westerners will have learned that they cannot interpret Western behavior from the perspective of Indian culture, and they will be better able, as a consequence, to interpret Western behavior the way other Westerners would.

Advice for Westerners

We have established that Indians communicate "no," deliver bad news, and give negative feedback in a number of ways Westerners do not use, do not recognize, and do not understand. Moreover, we have also established that while the resulting misinterpretations and misunderstandings are unintended and legitimate—that no one is *trying* to miscommunicate—these misunderstandings are still a major nuisance.

So what can Westerners and Indians who work together do to avoid these misunderstandings? Ultimately, there are only two ways out of this dilemma: Westerners can get better at reading Indians, or Indians can get better at talking like Westerners. Ideally, some of both would take place, with each side going to some lengths to understand and adapt to the communication style of the other. After all, when both sides move toward each other from opposite ends of the communication spectrum, they meet a lot sooner than if either side has to travel the entire distance.

Who Adjusts to Whom?

Indians and Westerners who work together, then, should certainly aspire to and work toward this noble compromise, but in many cases it will not be practical. This is because in most circumstances where Indians and Westerners interact, one is the majority or dominant culture and the other is the minority or secondary culture. And it is only natural in these cases for those from the minority group to have to shoulder the burden of learning about and adapting to those of the majority. In most cases, it is the Indians who will end up adapting to the Westerners.

We hasten to add that the reason the minority should adjust to the majority is not because the behavior of the majority is necessarily more logical, normal, or evolved; it is, rather, simply because there are a lot more people (which is why they're called the majority) behaving in this particular way in this particular workplace. As a result, it will be much easier—for *everyone*—if the behavior of the majority is established as the norm for this workplace. It will be easier for the Westerners (assuming they are the majority) because that's already how they behave, and easier for the Indians (assuming they are the minority) because it will take much longer for all those Westerners to get the hang of Indian culture than for a handful of Indians to figure the Westerners out. Needless to say, if the tables were turned and Westerners were working in India for Indian clients, then the burden would be on them to adapt to Indian culture. The whole question of who adapts to whom is not normally something Indians and Westerners ever have to discuss or decide; typically, it just happens.

In most of the offshore models, where Indian vendors are doing work for European and American clients or where Western companies are operating wholly owned subsidiaries in India, the Westerners stay in their country and interact with Indians by telephone, including regular conference calls, e-mail, and sometimes videoconferencing. In addition, there may be some Indians on site in the Western company's offices, and some European and American staff may travel from time to time to India on short visits. Typically, the Westerners will interact with a select group of Indians who serve in some kind of liaison capacity.

In these circumstances, where the Westerners work in their own culture, interacting most of the time with other Westerners like themselves and occasionally—at the most a few times a day—with select Indians (either in person on site or via phone or e-mail offshore), it is not realistic to expect that the Westerners are going to get very good at decoding Indian-style communication; they simply won't have enough exposure. It makes more sense that the Indians the Westerners are dealing with will somehow become better at Western-style communication. In the author's experience, most Indians who work in these arrangements readily accept this reality.

In *What's This India Business?*, Paul Davies has set forth three other reasons why it is usually the Indians who end up doing the heavy lifting (quite cheerfully, in most cases):

[I]t is necessary for [Westerners] to have a common conceptual basis with Indian businesspeople. At root, this is some form of Western understanding.

Put this way it seems arrogant, because it apparently places all the hard work on Indian business people again. Yet because of the global spread of Western business models and methods, the greater exposure of Indians to Western business than the other way around, and the influence of Western media, there is more chance for Indians to get inside Western minds than the reverse. (Davies, 66)

Coaching Indians

But that doesn't mean it's easy for Indians to communicate like Westerners —and more important, it doesn't mean the Westerners are off the cultural hook. While the burden of adjustment is indeed on the Indians in most cases, and while they cheerfully shoulder that burden, the Americans and Europeans involved in these ventures have a key role to play in helping Indians bridge the communication gap. If they are aware of this role and play it well, Westerners can dramatically shorten the time it takes for their Indian colleagues to begin communicating more like Westerners.

Indians *can* learn Western-style communication on their own, especially if they are working in a Western workplace, but they will learn it a lot faster, regardless of where they're located, if the experts (Westerners) help them. By acting as cultural coaches or mentors, Americans and Europeans can explain their workplace norms and expectations to their Indian colleagues, pointing out how they would like the Indians to communicate and, just as important, how the way Indians do communicate is often misinterpreted by Westerners. Indians often learn all these things the hard way, by making mistakes and being misunderstood by Westerners, but they can also learn them an easier way, from Westerners who explain ahead of time how communication happens in their country. This presupposes, of course, that the Westerners in question are aware of the key cultural differences in communication style and realize what mistakes Indians are likely to make and what advice they need to be given.

So how does this coaching work? What specifically can Americans and Europeans do to help Indians bridge the communication gap? We will consider suggestions for each of the big three problems we have discussed above: saying "no," delivering bad news, and giving negative feedback.

Coaching Indians to Say "No"   With regard to the varieties of the Indian "no," Westerners should explain to Indians that they, the Indians, need to be more direct or the Westerners will not understand them. Americans and Europeans need to clearly point out, with specific examples such as the two-person exchanges above, that all the various techniques Indians have of saying "no" will very rarely be interpreted as "no" by most Westerners. Indeed, not only will these messages not be interpreted as "no" by Westerners; they are more likely to be interpreted as "yes." This may be hard for some Indians to believe—as hard as it is for Westerners to believe that Indians think these things mean "no"—so Westerners may have to persist and give several examples.

Eventually Indians will begin to understand how these misinterpretations happen, or, even if they don't understand exactly *how* they come about, they will trust that Westerners know what they're talking about and take their word that these misinterpretations do in fact occur quite regularly. And Indians won't need any help understanding the potentially disastrous consequences that result when Westerners regularly mistake the Indian "no" for "yes." In short, Indians will be very open to and even eager for any advice about how they can keep these disasters from happening.

Here, then, is a list of the most common techniques Indians use to say "no" that Westerners may want to do some coaching about:

- The no-response response.
- Avoiding the question/changing the subject.

- The postponed answer.
- Repeating the question.
- Turning the question back on the speaker.
- Hesitation.
- The qualified or conditional "yes."

In general this coaching should focus on two key messages: (1) that these techniques will not be understood the way Indians think they will, and (2) that Indians will need to be much more explicit in delivering negative messages. In other words, Indians will have to learn how to be more direct. In talking with scores of Indians over the years, I have asked them what was the biggest single cultural adjustment they have had to make in working with people from the United States and Europe, and invariably Indians have responded with the same answer: We have had to learn to be very direct.

But coaching around directness is not just a matter of telling Indians they need to speak their minds, since from their point of view Indians *are* speaking their minds when they talk. When Indians use the techniques we have described here, they are in fact coming across loud and clear to other Indians; they are being quite direct *as directness is defined in Indian culture*. The problem is that Indian-style directness is more or less the exact equivalent of Western-style indirectness, and, we might add, vice versa: Western-style indirectness comes across as directness in Indian culture.

A graphic might make all this clearer.

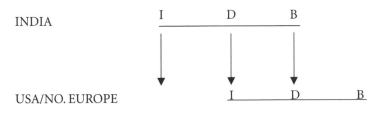

Figure 3.1 How Indians are perceived by Westerners.

In this graphic, "I" stands for indirect, "D" is direct, and "B" is blunt. Each culture has its own culturally correct versions of these three types of communication. Indians can be what Indians consider indirect (none of our examples have illustrated this), what Indians consider direct (all of our conversations are examples of this), and what Indians consider blunt. The same, of course, is true for Westerners, who can be what Westerners consider indirect, direct, and blunt.

But these three categories of communication all become relative as soon as one is talking to someone outside one's own culture. When Indians are being indirect, there is really no equivalent of that in Western culture (see left arrow in Figure 3-1); when Indians are being direct, that equates to Western indirectness (middle arrow; all of our two-person conversations are examples of this); and when Indians are being blunt and on the verge of rude, that's roughly the same as Western directness (right arrow).

And the same thing is true in reverse:

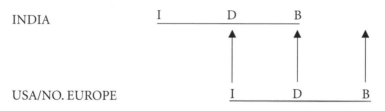

Figure 3.2 How Westerners are perceived by Indians.

When Westerners (left arrow) are being indirect—diplomatic, tactful, and pulling their punches—this is how Indians talk when they're being direct. When Westerners are being direct (middle arrow), neither tactful nor blunt, this is on the verge of impoliteness to Indians. And when Westerners are being blunt (right arrow), this is beyond the bounds of acceptable conversation in Indian culture.

Keeping all this in mind, let's look again at the single most important piece of coaching advice Westerners need to give to Indians: be more direct. As we have just explained, what Westerners mean by direct (D on the USA/No. Europe continuum) is what Indians would call blunt (B on the Indian continuum).

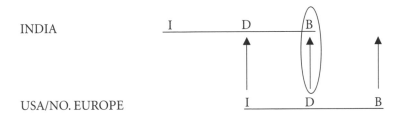

Figure 3.3 What it means to tell an Indian to be direct.

In short, when Westerners tell Indians they have to be more direct, they are in effect telling them that they have to be close to rude before colleagues in the United States and northern Europe will understand them. When Westerners coach Indians to be direct, they should make it clear that they mean *Western-style* directness. And they should be careful to add that they realize they are actually asking Indians to be blunt or even rude, and then reassure them that speaking this way is not considered rude in the United States and northern Europe.

Asking someone to be blunt is a different proposition from asking someone to be direct. Westerners should realize that just as it doesn't feel comfortable for them as they approach the blunt extreme of their continuum, it's going to feel very uncomfortable for Indians as they approach the blunt end of theirs, *even when Westerners assure Indians that they're not really being impolite.* It's not that Indians won't believe Westerners when they say this; it's just that it doesn't feel right.

When Westerners understand this, then they will understand the need for three other pieces that should go along with the coaching advice to Indians to be more direct

1. Be sure to repeat the advice several times so that Indians will know you're serious.
2. Give Indians plenty of time to get used to being what they regard as impolite.
3. Be sure to give immediate and strong positive feedback as soon as you see the least sign of Indians doing what you have asked.

The first time Raj says "I'm not sure that will work" instead of "Do you think that will work?" be sure to praise him highly and thank him for doing what you know is not easy for him. When you do this a few times, Indians will begin to believe that their "rude" is really not your "rude," and it will become increasingly easy for them say "no" the Western way.

To recap, the basic steps in coaching Indians to be more direct are as follows:

1. Explain that you want them to be more direct.
2. Explain why: describe how their version of direct actually comes across as quite indirect to Westerners and is therefore often misunderstood.
3. Explain that what you mean by being "direct" actually means being blunt and close to impolite in Indian culture, *but that Westerners do not take it that way.*
4. Repeat the advice to be more direct several times, with the necessary reassurances that it's not interpreted as rude.
5. Be patient and give Indians some time to get comfortable with being impolite.
6. Give immediate and lots of positive feedback whenever Indians do manage to be more direct.

If we go back to our original two examples: Marian should explain to Kumar that he can actually say that it will be "difficult" or words to that effect to move up the date for the systems test, and Bill should explain to

Anu that if Tuesday is not a good time for the tour, she can say that Tuesday "won't work" and propose another day. Indians will think they *have* said these things, of course, because that would be true if they were talking to another Indian. But they aren't, and Westerners will not understand.

Coaching for Bad News and Negative Feedback   The bad news problem is in essence just a subset of the "saying no" problem in that the core dilemma is the same: telling clients, customers, or one's boss something they may not want to hear and thereby upsetting the harmony between the parties. And so it is done very delicately, so delicately, as we've seen, that Westerners don't actually receive the bad news until it's too late.

The coaching advice for the bad news problem involves the same six steps as for saying "no," with only minor adjustments:

1. Explain that you want them to deliver bad news more forcefully.
2. Explain why: show how their ways of describing bad news do not make the news sound bad to Westerners, who therefore see no cause for concern or any need to act.
3. Explain that what you mean by being "forceful" may sound extreme or exaggerated to Indians but is not taken that way by Westerners.
4. Repeat the advice to be more forceful several times, with the necessary reassurances that it's not seen as exaggerated.
5. Be patient and give Indians some time to get comfortable with delivering bad news more forcefully.
6. Give immediate and lots of positive feedback whenever Indians do manage to be more forceful.

Negative feedback is also a delicate matter and poses the same essential dilemma as the other two issues (telling people what they don't want to hear), but it also raises the added specter of causing loss of face. It's uncomfortable enough having to disappoint and perhaps frustrate people by saying no or delivering bad news, but it's even more painful to risk embarrassing people by criticizing their ideas or their performance. As we've seen, Indians solve the problem in the usual way, with circumlocutions and innuendo (from the Western perspective, that is), but they are too clever by half: in commenting by means of withholding comment, they succeed only in making *no* comment as far as most Americans and Europeans are concerned.

Coaching around this may not be as successful as in the other two areas because to the Indian way of thinking any unfortunate consequences of Westerners not understanding their negative feedback might very well be preferable to the unfortunate consequences of embarrassing their Western colleagues with that same feedback and causing offense. Westerners can try, encouraging Indians to be more direct (following the six steps listed above), but they should not be as sanguine about their prospects of changing this particular behavior as they were with saying "no" and giving bad news. This is especially the case if the feedback has to be given in front of other people, such as at a meeting; Indians will not do this, and it would normally be a waste of time to coach them in this respect.

Getting the Bad News Sooner

Besides coaching, another technique Westerners can use to uncover bad news before it's too late is to set up more frequent milestones or check-ins with your Indian colleagues. If you usually check in once a week with a team to see how they're progressing and if they're still on schedule, you might want to check in twice as often with an Indian team. This is not because checking in more often will cause the Indians to suddenly be forthcoming and tell you they're behind schedule, but because the more often you hear the subtle hints that something may be wrong the better the chances that sooner or later the message will come through.

The Indian Cultural Broker

Another technique groups or teams use, sometimes by default and sometimes by design, is to use one or more Indians as point people for communication between East and West. These are usually senior Indians who are onshore at the client site and who have had a lot of experience with Westerners. Westerners communicate through these individuals to the other Indians who are working for them, and, more important, those Indians in turn communicate to the Westerners they work for through these cultural middle men and women. In this way, the theory goes, Westerners don't really have to figure out Indian-style communication; they just rely on their brokers to translate into Western-style communication whatever it is the Indians are really saying.

There is much to recommend this approach in those circumstances where it is appropriate, but both sides are somewhat naïve if they believe this approach makes the cultural issue disappear altogether. For one thing, even the most Westernized Indians are still probably more Indian than they are Western, and for another it is usually not possible or even desirable to route all communications between both sides through just a few individuals. Nevertheless, it is definitely true that the more attuned Indians in these liaison positions are to cultural differences, the better they can serve as honest brokers.

Five Behavior Changes for Westerners

Coaching Indians to change their behavior is probably the quickest route to bridging the East-West communications gap, and time, after all, is of the essence in much of the work performed by these partnerships. Coaching has its drawbacks, however, the most obvious is that coaches have no control over the ultimate outcome of their coaching; they can advise, cajole, persuade, and otherwise try to influence the Indians they work with, but in the end it is the Indians who have to change. There are, however, certain changes Westerners can make to their *own* behavior to improve their chances of understanding Indians, changes that are entirely within their control. They can do these things at the same time as they coach Indians, thereby doubling their chances for success.

Check for Understanding   Westerners who are worried that they may have misinterpreted Indians can employ the simple expedient of asking them. If you hang up the phone or walk out of a meeting wondering whether you actually understood what the Indians were telling you—if you're worried, in other words, that you have just been in a conversation like those re-created in this chapter—then sit down and write an e-mail describing what it is you think the Indians told you, and then send it off and ask the Indians to verify your understanding. If what you have written is not what the Indians meant, if your fears are justified and you have in fact misinterpreted them, and the Indians are sitting there reading your erroneous conclusions, they're not going to sit by and let you persist in your delusions. They will write back and, politely and tactfully, correct your misinterpretations. If you then misread that communication, then you may be beyond help. In many cases, incidentally, Indians will beat you to the punch, writing their own e-mails laying out what was just discussed or agreed to and asking if you have any corrections.

Don't Telegraph the Answer You Want   Another technique to improve communication is to be careful not to telegraph the answer you want when you're talking to Indians. The number-one communications priority of most Indians, after all, is to say what they think the other person wants to hear, so if you indicate in any way what it is you'd like to hear, don't be surprised if Indians oblige. Indians are so good at this that they can usually figure out the response you're looking for just by your body language or the general direction of the conversation. Here are some of the more obvious triggers that will alert Indians immediately to the answer you're looking for:

"Is there any way you could get that done by Friday?

"We're still on schedule, right?

"That should be possible, shouldn't it?

"That won't take you long, will it?

"You guys know how to do that, don't you?"

"I was hoping . . . .What do you think?"

"You probably have some experience in this area, I guess?"

"That should work, don't you think?"

Ask Indians What They Think   A related technique in this context is to consider withholding your idea or suggestion about how something should be done or your opinion of something and to first ask Indians what they think. If you make a proposal and *then* ask Indians how they feel about it or offer your opinion on something and *then* ask for theirs, Indians will interpret this as a declaration of how you would like to proceed and will regard your asking for their response as pure politeness. They will feel boxed in, in short, and will almost always accept your most admirable suggestion and agree with your most excellent opinion.

Even when you hold back and ask Indians how they would execute the task or solve the problem in question, their first response will almost always be to ask you what you think, especially if they are junior to you. This is only polite, after all. In this case, you should resist the temptation to answer, thereby demonstrating that you really do want to hear their views (and aren't just being polite yourself), and then most Indians will feel comfortable responding. The bottom line here is simple: If you truly want to know what Indians think, don't begin by telling them what you think.

If you truly want to know what Indians think, don't begin by telling them what you think.

Seek Out One-on-One Conversations   As we've already noted, Indians are especially careful about what they say in any kind of group setting, such as a meeting or a conference call. Simply stated, meetings are such minefields when it comes to saying things that could cause a loss of face, either someone else's or one's own, that many things just can't be said at a meeting, or else they have to be said with such care and tact that as far as most Westerners are concerned, they might as well not have been said. (See chapter 7 for more details.) Westerners who have trouble understanding Indians in the best of circumstances, therefore, are going to have even more trouble in public settings where Indians are really being subtle. Consequently, they should seek Indians out for one-on-one conversations whenever possible, as difficult and delicate matters can be discussed much more openly one-on-one.

Get to Know the Indians You Work With   Ultimately, people from group-oriented cultures are the most comfortable with people from their group. Given their druthers, in other words, collectivists would much prefer to limit their contact to fellow members of their collective, to the people they know they can rely on and trust, no matter what. This is not possible in the modern world, naturally, but the instinct lives on. Westerners don't belong to an Indian's primary group, of course, but if they make the effort to build rapport and establish close personal relationships with their Indian colleagues, they can in effect become honorary members of an Indian's collective and enjoy its many benefits. Once Indians regard someone as one of their group, they are likely to be more relaxed, trusting, and open around that person. With the people they know well, Indians are more likely to speak their mind, disagree, and even give negative feedback. This is only human nature; most people are more comfortable around the people they know. But this is especially true for collectivist cultures where the distinction between the people one knows—one's ingroup—and everyone else, one's outgroup, is particularly acute. The time spent getting to know personally the Indians one works with will pay great dividends.

"Work gets done by people," observes Mary Lacity at the University of Missouri at St Louis,

> It doesn't get done by processes . . . It's [all] about building the social capital between the customer and the [Indian] supplier. It's not only about knowing the business; it's knowing who is in the business. Then knowledge transfer occurs. You develop better relationships with your supplier and your quality goes up. (Overby, 8)

Rude Westerners?

Our focus in this chapter has been on how Indians come across to Westerners, but it will not have escaped the reader that there must also be problems in the opposite direction. There are, but the difficulty is not so much that Indians don't understand what Westerners are saying but that they understand them all too well.

We did not linger over this at the time, but the other message of Figure 3-2 is how Indians perceive Western-style communication. And it's not a pretty picture. Western directness (middle arrow), as the figure shows, is very close to being blunt by Indian standards, and Western bluntness (right arrow) has no equivalent on the Indian chart. Most of the time, then, when Westerners are communicating with Indians, they evidently come across as blunt and on the verge of rude.

But is this true? Is this actually how Westerners are perceived by Indians? It *should* be true, if our figure is accurate, and it does seem to be true initially, but then something apparently happens, for it is in fact relatively rare to meet Indians who complain about rude Westerners, and this is not because Indians are just being polite.

What accounts for this anomaly? What seems to happen is that when Indians first talk with an American or a German or a Finn (but usually not with the British, who tend to be less direct than Americans and other northern Europeans), these Westerners do come across as abrupt, curt, and somewhat impolite. But then Indians begin to observe these Americans interacting with other Americans, and they can't help but notice that these other Americans don't become offended when their colleagues talk to them like this. Indians quickly see, in short, that what is rude to Indians is apparently not rude at all to Americans, and they realize as a result that Americans are probably not trying to be offensive but just don't realize how they're coming across to Indians. They may still sound abrupt to Indians, but they are not judged negatively for that. We should note, incidentally, that Indians who do not have the opportunity to observe these "blunt" Westerners interacting with each other are much more likely to feel that Westerners are rude.

When Westerners venture into their own blunt (B) zone, as shown in Figure 3-1, they are in uncharted territory as far as Indians are concerned; Indians just don't talk this way under any circumstances. When Westerners do this, even Indians who know better—who know that they should regard these comments as blunt but not beyond blunt—are likely to take offense. Usually they become very quiet in such cases and may simply shut down, as most people do when confronted with behavior considered inappropriate in polite society. Westerners would do well to stay away from their blunt zone as much as possible.

Advice for Indians

Indian readers who have reached this point can probably imagine what we're going to say here. After all, what Indians need to do to communicate more successfully with Westerners is implicit in and virtually the mirror image of our advice to Westerners on how to work better with Indians. Here, then, are a few summary points for Indians to keep in mind when they work with people from the United States and northern Europe:

- Westerners do not value group harmony as highly as Indians do, so you do not have to worry so much about coming across as impolite or disrespectful.
- Westerners worry much less about face than Indians do, so it is more difficult to embarrass them.
- Remember that "yes" is interpreted as a positive response—not just "I hear you"—by most Westerners.
- It's perfectly acceptable—indeed, it is quite often necessary—to use the word "no" with Westerners.
- Westerners do not interpret the absence of "yes" as meaning "no"; they need to hear the words "no," "not," or some other type of negation.
- Westerners typically do not assign *any* meaning to what is not said.
- By and large, Westerners want you to "speak your mind," by which they mean saying what you actually think, *not what you think the Westerner wants to hear.*

- Qualified or conditional responses—possibly, maybe, I think so—do not mean "no" to Westerners; if anything, they are closer to "yes."
- To communicate bad news—we're behind schedule, something is not possible, we need help—you need to use these words exactly or something very similar.
- To communicate negative feedback you must *say something negative,* not merely refrain from saying anything positive.
- When Westerners are being what you consider impolite and rude, this is almost never what they intend, and they would be quite embarrassed to know this is how they were coming across to you.

General advice:

- Observe closely what the Westerners are doing and listen to how they talk to each other; this is probably the right way to behave in their culture and, therefore, how they're expecting *you* to behave.
- Don't force yourself to adopt Western behaviors that make you feel very uncomfortable; try to find a compromise between what you would do in India and what Westerners are expecting, something you can live with.

We conclude these two chapters on communication by reminding readers of how we began them: not with a consideration of the main topic, Indian communication style, but with an explanation of a key aspect of culture: the Indian self-concept. Our point was to establish that behavior, in this instance the way Indians communicate, is not arbitrary or capricious, something people make up on the spot and can easily change. Behavior springs from deep within the subconscious and is the result of layers of cultural conditioning laid down at an early age and continuously reinforced by years of experience.

To change behavior, therefore, is not a simple matter—even when people understand the need to change and are willing to change. It is, rather, a slow and gradual process that requires overriding deep-rooted instincts and closely monitoring one's everyday actions. In short, behavior change calls for patience and understanding *on all sides*.

Best Practices: Communication Style

A summary of the main advice to
Westerners given in this chapter

- ➤ Never accept the word "yes" by itself for an answer; listen to what the person says next.
- ➤ Don't confuse the Indian head wobble, tilting the head to one side and then to the other, for the "no" gesture; it actually means I'm listening or even "yes."
- ➤ Try to listen for the various ways Indians **say "no"** by:
  - Not responding at all.
  - Avoiding the question/changing the subject.
  - Postponing the response: Can I get back to you?
  - Repeating your question.
  - Turning the question back on the speaker.
  - Hesitating before they answer.
  - Giving a qualified or conditional "yes".
- ➤ Listen for how Indians say they're **behind schedule** by:
  - Repeatedly bringing up the subject of the schedule/deadline.
  - Saying that the schedule is inconvenient or ambitious.
  - Asking if the deadline is still good for you.
  - Asking if *all* parts of the work need to be done by the deadline.
  - Mentioning that part of the project is taking longer than expected.
  - Mentioning that some parts of the project *are* on schedule.
  - Asking if members of another team are busy or observing that they don't seem to be.
  - Mentioning how much overtime they are working/how late they are working each day.
  - Mentioning that some people are coming in on the weekends.
  - Pointing out how another team was recently given more time to finish their project.

- Listen for how Indians say that something is **not possible/they're not available** by:
  - Answering with any kind of qualifier: That might be possible. We'll try our best.
  - Postponing the answer: Let me ask my team. Can I get back to you on that?
  - Not answering/responding with a question: Do you think that's possible?
  - Making references to how busy they are.
  - Initially agreeing to the request and then bringing it up/asking about it again later.
- Listen for how Indians **ask for help** by:
  - Repeatedly mentioning how busy they are.
  - Mentioning that something is taking longer than expected.
  - Implying that a deadline might be missed (hoping you will then ask why).
  - Mentioning that something was more complicated/more involved than they thought.
  - Talking about another team that recently needed and received help.
  - Talking about a time in the past when they received help in a very similar situation.
- Listen for how Indians express **negative feedback/criticism** of your suggestion/proposal by:
  - Avoiding any response/dodging the question.
  - Repeating your suggestion.
  - A loud silence.
  - Suggesting an alternative (without commenting on your idea).
  - Asking your opinion of your own idea/proposal.
  - Damning with faint praise: praising a small, insignificant part of your proposal.
- Encourage and coach Indians to be more direct with you, explaining that what sounds rude to them is only interpreted as direct by Westerners. After encouraging Indians to be direct, then:
  - Repeat the advice a few times.
  - Give them some time to become comfortable with being direct.
  - Give immediate positive feedback as soon as they show any signs of being more direct.

- Schedule more frequent check-ins or updates to increase your chances of hearing about delays or problems sooner.
- Use a cultural middleman where possible, an Indian who is more Western and who can translate to Westerners what other Indians are really saying.
- Check for understanding: If you're not sure you have understood something, send an e-mail describing what you think Indians told you and ask them to verify it.
- Don't telegraph the answer you want: Be careful not to include in your statement the answer you're looking for: That should be possible, don't you think? You can do that, can't you?
- Seek out one-on-one conversations; Indians can be much more frank one-on-one than in group settings such as meetings.
- If you want to know what Indians think, don't begin by telling them what you think.
- Build rapport and establish good personal relationships with the Indians you work with.

General Advice:

Remember that when you misunderstand something Indians have told you, it was never their intention or desire that you not understand them.

Management East and Management West

The hierarchical nature of Indian society demands that there is a boss and that the boss should be seen to be a boss.

Gitanjali Kolanad

A number of writers have observed that the role model for Indian managers is the father or oldest male in the Indian household, and the model for manager-subordinate relations is the deeply hierarchical nature of the Indian extended family system. Indeed, since the majority of Indian businesses are privately held and family owned, in many cases the head of the household and the head of the company are one and the same individual. There is no doubt much more to the Indian style of management than what bosses and subordinates learn and practice in the home, but the extended family dynamic is the breeding ground of so many Indian cultural attitudes and so much typically Indian behavior that it is the essential starting point for explaining how managers and subordinates behave in India. "The family is the nucleus," Stanley Wolpert has written, "the matrix, the model from which all that is Indian grows, often in direct imitation or emulation of what is learned, expected, and found there" (Wolpert 2005, 136).

Westerners need to understand Indian-style management for two reasons: how managers behave in India is what Indian subordinates are used to and what they will therefore be expecting from Western managers; and, even more important, how Indian subordinates relate to and interact with Indian managers is how they're going to relate to and interact with Western managers. But given that the American and northern European styles of management are in fact quite different from the Indian style, the stage is once again set for considerable cross-cultural confusion, as Indian subordinates and Western bosses repeatedly discover that their assumptions about good management are not mutual and that their expectations of how each should interact with the other are wildly misaligned.

We should mention in this context that while Westerners in many offshore ventures may not officially manage all or even most of the Indians they work with—indeed, strictly speaking, they may not manage any of them—Indians nevertheless tend to view most Westerners in offshore ventures as "managers" in the broader sense that they are the people who come from the client organization, from the company the Indians work *for* or partner *with*, the entity calling the shots, and they are, therefore, the people who need to be pleased (and Indians, by implication, are the ones who need to do the pleasing). For the purposes of this chapter, then, when we speak of managers, we mean Westerners regardless of whether they actually manage any Indians, and when we speak of subordinates, we mean Indians irrespective of their relationship to the Westerners they work with.

Management East

In the previous chapter, we noted the deeply hierarchical nature of the Indian extended family, a well-defined pecking order based on age and to a lesser extent gender, with all members knowing their place and their role, the entire edifice ruled over by the oldest male in a position of undisputed authority at the very top. This dynamic goes a long way toward explaining the central fact about manager-subordinate interaction in India: that it is fundamentally a relationship of unequals, of superiors and subordinates. "Once a hierarchy is established," Jai Sinha writes in his book *Work Culture in the Indian Context,*

"Once a hierarchy is established, juniors yield to seniors on every conceivable occasion."

juniors yield to seniors on every conceivable occasion. They leave their seat for a senior in a crowded bus or train; stand up when he enters the office; open doors for him; refrain from smoking or drinking alcohol in his presence even on social occasions; speak humbly and politely; do not disagree strongly; and would rather withdraw from a situation that is likely to force a confrontation with their senior.

Indian teams do not consist of equals; they consist of unequals . . . . (1990, 35)

All of which puts India squarely in the camp of the so-called high-power distance cultures.

The Boss Is the Boss (High Power Distance)

In his famous study of workplace culture referred to in the previous chapter, Dutch sociologist Geert Hofstede coined the phrase "power distance" to describe the attitude people in different cultures hold toward the distribution of power and influence and, inevitably, toward how power is regarded and exercised by those in authority. In high power distance cultures, people accept and are comfortable with an unequal distribution of power and authority, and there is accordingly a wider gap (or distance) between those with and without power. These cultures tend to be more authoritarian and autocratic, leaders hold on closely to their power and are unlikely to delegate authority and responsibility, and the chain of command is scrupulously respected. In low power distance cultures, by contrast, people are uncomfortable with an unequal distribution of power, and there is a corresponding tendency to minimize the power gap, with leaders much more likely to delegate authority and responsibility, and subordinates more likely to go around the chain of command in certain situations.

In his survey of workplace practices in 60 countries, Hofstede measured power distance (among other topics) and published his findings in his groundbreaking 1984 book *Culture's Consequences: International Differences in Work-Related Values* (later updated in 1991 as *Cultures and Organizations: Software of the Mind*). The power distance scores for India and for the United States and selected northern European countries are given in the table below, with a high score indicating a high power distance culture. The scores ranged from a low of 11 (Austria) to a high of 104 (Malaysia), with a mean of 46.5.

India 77	Great Britain 35
USA 40	Netherlands 38
Australia 36	New Zealand 22
Denmark 18	Norway 31
Finland 33	Sweden 31
Germany 35	Switzerland 34

Source: Hofstede, 1991, p. 53

In his analysis of his findings, Hofstede observed that a spread of 10 points or more between any two countries would be likely to result in significant cultural differences in workplace attitudes and practices. Not surprisingly, then, a spread of almost 40 points, such as that between Americans and Indians and between the English and Indians, is going to raise serious havoc when bosses from the West try to manage subordinates from the East.

Superiors and Subordinates

As it plays out in the workplace, the essence of the authoritarian management style—the superior/subordinate dynamic—is the need for subordinates to defer to their boss, to always be polite and respectful, and never to openly offend, challenge, correct, or otherwise disagree with their superior. It would not be an overstatement to say that when Indian subordinates interact with their boss, their overriding objective is to demonstrate their deference. The interaction will naturally serve other more practical purposes—to discuss an issue, to exchange information, to get instructions, to give an update—but these must all be pursued within the constraints of being polite and always showing respect towards one's seniors. If this is not possible in a particular situation, then it is the purpose that gets compromised but never the politeness.

This should not be surprising, for in the superior/subordinate dynamic the personal and professional well-being, the continued good fortune—in short, the career—of the subordinate depend in large part on the sufferance and favor of the superior. Simply put, those who enjoy the boss's favor thrive in the Indian work environment; those who do not, struggle. And the surest way to win favor is never to offend or disagree with those above you.

The surest way to win favor is never to offend or disagree with those above you.

In the Indian workplace, deference and subservience are not the sad lot of the meek and downtrodden; they are a strategy for survival. "The more one gives—and gives selflessly—the more one gets," Jai Sinha has written, and he goes on to point out how the unequal power dynamic actually serves the interests of both parties:

> The superior "gives" in terms of affection, nurturance, blessing (*kripa*), and the subordinates in terms of loyalty, submissiveness, and obedience . . . . There is no resistance and no conflict. The less powerful seeks direction . . . and the more powerful obliges by providing a lead. The powerful feels great and the less powerful blossoms in the reflected power of the powerful.

The subordinates sense the game and adopt [a] sophisticated strategy. They seemingly depend on the superior, run to him for help, seek his guidance and blessings, and overly show submissiveness. But these are actually tactics for ingratiation, meant to serve their end. (1990, 41)

Conformity   The superior/subordinate dynamic and the strong collectivist preference for group harmony discussed in the previous two chapters combine to create another dominant feature of the Indian workplace: the instinct to conform. If keeping your head down is the way to gain the boss's favor and keeping the group happy the best way to protect yourself, then it's no wonder Indians are always looking to see which way the wind is blowing. The Indian instinct is for compromise, reconciliation, and playing it safe, for never having an opinion on something until one knows the opinions of others. Ask an Indian what he or she thinks of something, and nine times out of ten the response will be to put the question back to you.

Needless to say, this is not fertile ground for rocking the boat—for creativity, originality, or innovation. Indians can and do innovate, but they face far greater obstacles and receive much less encouragement than their counterparts in the West. "Conformity to authority, to the family, to the [caste] becomes the first law of Indian life," Wolpert observes,

and a major limiting factor to creative growth, radical change, or independent initiative. India's multifaceted search for concessions, its overall impulse toward finding some means of preserving unity, maintaining traditions, integrating diverse points of view, reconciling differences, and harmonizing polarities are public extensions of joint-family life . . . [resulting in] the comforting stability, the security—and all the conformist limitations and modern Indian weaknesses as well. (2005, 136)

Obedience   Another closely related quality bred by the family dynamic is almost automatic obedience to authority. Indians obey first and ask questions later—if then. From a very early age Indians learn that the easiest way to make adults happy and, not coincidentally, to get one's own way, is to always do what people in charge tell you (or at least to *say* you will). As we saw in the previous chapter, this explains in part why Indians always say "yes" no matter what the question and, indeed, often before they've even heard the entire question. They know they're going to say "yes" anyway, so why wait until the question has actually been completed? "Indians for the most part," Wolpert continues, "are an obedient, deferential people, accepting of 'higher' authority even when vocal in their objection to what they may view as grossly unfair or intolerable restrictions, regulations, or orders. Such obedience is family-inculcated" (2005, 134).

Face

Another key dimension of management Indian-style is saving face, which we first encountered in the previous two chapters on communication. We defined face and its workings in some detail in those chapters, so we will confine ourselves here to looking at face only in the context of the manager-subordinate relationship. The face we are talking about here, incidentally, is usually that of the boss and only occasionally that of the subordinate.

Simply stated, the face of one's superior must be protected at all costs.

If, as noted earlier, saving face is an important consideration in almost all Indian social and workplace interactions, then it is paramount in superior/subordinate interactions; simply stated, the face of one's superior must be protected at all costs. This is why deferring and being polite and respectful to one's boss take on such significance in the Indian workplace. If we look at even a partial list of the ways the boss (and seniors in general) can lose face, we begin to understand a number of the typical behaviors of Indian subordinates. Bosses can lose face when subordinates:

- Challenge or question something the boss says.
- Disagree with something the boss says.
- Correct the boss in front of others.
- Act as if they know more than their boss.
- Criticize, even by implication, something the boss says or does.
- Answer a question (from someone else) in front of the boss.
- Fail to inform the boss about something.
- Make even routine decisions without informing the boss.

The first three of these actions—questioning, disagreeing with, and correcting the boss—need to be done in the normal course of work in any culture, and Indians have their ways of doing them, but they are rarely done in front of others and almost never done overtly. Indeed, the way these delicate tasks are carried out would not even register to a watching Westerner, and when they are done *to* a Western manager, as we will see below, he usually doesn't realize what is happening.

Management West

The foregoing, then, is the management style Indians are steeped in, to which their instincts are finely attuned, and the dictates of which they are used to following. And the first thing many readers will notice is that all this bears little or no resemblance to how Westerners manage. Not all Westerners manage the same way, of course, even within the same Western country, to say nothing of in different Western countries. But there are enough general similarities between the management style of the United States and the northern tier of European countries—ways the management styles in these countries, different as they are, are still more like each other than they are like the Indian style—there are enough similarities that we can speak of a "Western" style for the purposes of the present discussion.

First Among Equals (Low Power Distance)

The biggest cultural difference is that the American and northern European management style is much less autocratic and authoritarian. Bosses are in charge and subordinates do their bidding in these countries too, but it is nothing like the relationship of unequals described earlier. Indeed, a manager in the West is often referred to as "first among equals," with as much emphasis on "equals" as on "first." Managers may indeed be superior, but they know better than to act that way.

The biggest cultural difference is that the American and northern European management style is much less autocratic and authoritarian.

As noted earlier, Western management style is low power distance, where authority is exercised with restraint and power is worn lightly. "Power is one of the last dirty words," one of the leading American management gurus has observed about the American workplace. "It is easier to talk about money—and much easier to talk about sex—than it is to talk about power. People who have it deny it; people who want it do not want to appear too hungry for it; and people who engage in its machinations do so secretly" (Kanter 1997, 135).

Two other cross-cultural observers have made a similar observation about the exercise of power in the United States

In egalitarian American culture companies talk of the participative workplace where employees are empowered to control their own jobs and destinies. The idea of having power over someone, or, worse yet, being under someone's power, makes most Americans vaguely uncomfortable . . . . In . . . Latin cultures, power is acknowledged and spoken of openly. High-level people use their power freely, usually to their own advantage, and are respectfully deferred to by those they control. (Asselin and Mastron, 2001, 200)

One could easily substitute India for the phrase "Latin cultures" in this quotation and it would still be accurate.

For the most part, as this writer has observed elsewhere, Americans don't like to manage—or to be managed—and much about the American workplace is set up precisely to keep the genie (i.e., power) in the bottle, set up, in short, so that workers never have to witness the ugly spectacle of bosses throwing their weight around. When a boss *does* have to throw his or her weight around, then something has gone terribly wrong. In the United States, the best managers are those who manage least.

In the so-called Anglo cultures (the United Kingdom, Canada, Australia, and New Zealand), it has likewise been observed that "superiors tend to be approachable, their subordinates are more willing to risk questioning what they are told . . . [and] it is easier for managers to delegate and decentralize" (Hickson and Pugh 1995, 51).

For their part the northern European cultures (Germany, the Netherlands, and the Scandinavian countries) are among the lowest of low power distance cultures (see Table on page 82), where "employees do not regard people in authority as remote beings whose word ought to be accepted without question; they expect to be consulted about decisions which affect them . . . [and] they are not afraid to express disagreement with their managers" (Hickson and Pugh, 93).

Obedience and conformity, two other stalwarts of Indian-style management, do not loom large in the Western workplace. Subordinates are as likely to be consulted about decisions as they are to be informed of them, and "thinking outside the box," as being creative and original is sometimes called, is encouraged and rewarded. In the West, a subordinate who is subservient, deferential, and ingratiating toward the manager is immediately suspect, certainly in the eyes of fellow subordinates but usually in those of the boss as well.

Westerners also don't lose much sleep over the other great factor in Indian management: the concept of face. Indeed, compared to the role face plays in Indian culture, it is hardly a factor at all in Western society. People from Boston or Bonn don't enjoy being embarrassed any more than people from Bangalore, of course, and don't deliberately set out to cause offense or make others look bad, but it takes much more to make a Westerner look bad than an Indian, and there aren't nearly as many ways to bring it about.

Finally, we should mention in closing that there will be some Western bosses who do not act anything like the typical manager described in this section. That is not because we've got our facts wrong, but because there is a range of management styles in the West—as, no doubt, there also is in India—from very hands-off to extremely hands-on, and we have described those managers who occupy the middle ground. They are most likely the majority, but there are probably some very colorful characters lurking at each of the extremes.

With this overview to guide us, we will now look at how these general differences in East/West management style play out in real situations in the workplace.

The Deference Syndrome

Hierarchy pervades Hindu society and culture, and [Indian] hierarchical relationships . . . are [quite] different from Western relationships.

A. Roland

If we combine the behaviors mandated by the superior/subordinate and face-saving dynamics and put the resulting style of management up against the Western model, the glaring differences explain most of what happens—and almost all of what goes *wrong*—when Americans and Europeans supervise Indians. In this chapter we will examine the fallout from this cultural misalignment and offer advice for how to bridge the gap that inevitably opens when West tries to manage East.

The Empowerment Problem

The Indian manager's instinct is to hold on to power rather than to share it with subordinates. Many observers have remarked that Indians often delegate responsibility and authority on paper but rarely in practice. Or, as more than one Indian has told me, bosses may delegate responsibility but they don't usually delegate authority. And they almost never give what Westerners call blanket authority.

Whether or not Indian bosses really empower their subordinates, one thing is certain: subordinates know better than to *act* as if they're empowered. This is most apparent in the common practice of Indian subordinates always checking with their bosses before making decisions or otherwise acting on things that have explicitly been delegated to them. To the Indian way of thinking, this is just common courtesy, showing respect by tacitly acknowledging the manager's prerogative to be regularly informed of and approve what subordinates are doing. There is more ritual to this than substance, in that Indian bosses usually just go along with whatever the subordinate was planning to do anyway, but checking in is not entirely *pro forma* in the sense that an Indian boss would certainly take note (and not a positive note) if a subordinate did not check in. Or, to put it another way, checking in *is* in fact *pro forma*, but form and appearance matter almost as much as substance in Indian culture.

Whether or not Indian bosses really empower their subordinates, one thing is certain: subordinates know better than to *act* as if they're empowered.

The problem that quickly develops here is that Western bosses *do* empower and delegate—responsibility *and* authority, on paper *and* in reality—and they don't expect to be consulted about those matters they have turned over to their subordinates. Indeed, they don't want to be consulted about those things, which is why they have delegated them to begin with, and they do not recognize any prerogatives regarding matters they have delegated. In a survey conducted in India and the United States, subordinates were asked whether or not they wanted "very close supervision" from their boss. Only 15 percent of Americans answered "yes," as compared with 85 percent of Indians (Adler, 139). Micro-management, in other words, is not a pejorative term in India.

I was once called by a senior vice president of a manufacturing company in a Western country whose plant managers were upset with their new boss, a well-known Indian industrialist who had recently acquired the company. The managers, who were used to almost complete autonomy in running their plants, were having a hard time adjusting to the probing phone calls, the endless and intrusive requests for information, and the introduction of quarterly performance reviews (they had previously been annual) by the new owner. They also took great exception to the way the new Indian boss "ordered them around" and generally interpreted his behavior as condescending and indicative of a serious lack of trust. When I explained that this was normal management behavior in Indian culture, the vice president was relieved to know that he had a cultural problem on his hands rather than a personality problem.

Going Through the Boss

Probably the most common problem the empowerment difference causes in the workplace is when Westerners try to deal directly with subordinates on an Indian team without going through the Indian boss, even concerning very routine matters. Not surprisingly, subordinates who have not been empowered are not comfortable acting without the knowledge and concurrence of their manager, and they would typically try to avoid responding to any contact that did not go through the chain of command. If they received an e-mail sent directly to them, for example, requesting some information, asking their views on something, or asking them to do something, they would typically either not answer or would show the e-mail to their manager.

If they were approached in person by a Westerner and asked to do something or asked their opinion of something, they might try to stall until they could alert their superior, dodge the request somehow, or put the Westerner in touch with their boss. An American woman told me how she e-mailed all the members of a newly hired team in India to ask them for their employee identification numbers and did not get an answer. She e-mailed them a second time and again got no reply, but on the third try she received an e-mail back from the team's boss (whom she had not e-mailed) saying he was collecting the information she had asked for and would be forwarding it. Another Western client told me that after she had trained an Indian team at a call center on a new procedure, she asked the participants for their feedback and any suggestions for improving the training. The participants said very little, but the next day she got an e-mail from the group's team leader saying he understood she had asked his team for feedback on her training and indicating that he would consult his team and get back to her with their suggestions.

For related reasons, Indians who work directly for a Western boss will want to check with him or her before doing the most routine tasks, including tasks that have explicitly been delegated. Another American manager told me that every time an Indian man she worked with offshore, nine and a half hours away in New Delhi, wanted to take his dinner break, he asked her (via instant messaging) if it was OK. She told him it wasn't necessary to ask, but he insisted it was "because I'm your subordinate." Eventually he did stop asking for permission but still routinely notified her when he was going on break and what time he would return. When Indian subordinates routinely check in with a Western manager, thinking they're being polite and respectful, they're actually annoying the manager, who considers it a waste of time to have to deal with matters he or she has delegated.

Westerners are used to contacting subordinates directly, since they assume that within reason subordinates can make their own decisions and exercise whatever authority has been delegated to them. When Indian subordinates are reluctant to act on their own, this surprises Westerners, who then start to wonder if the Indians lack confidence, are afraid of their bosses, or just don't want to be helpful.

Respecting the Chain of Command

Indians naturally assume the same norm applies in the West, so they will typically insist on checking with the Western manager before approaching subordinates about anything, even, incidentally, when Indians know the boss has delegated this particular responsibility. The Indian simply wants to show respect to the boss, of course, and also assumes (wrongly) that the subordinate won't want to act until the boss has been consulted.

An American female manager once told me about an Indian man she had been working with for two months on a software project (someone who did not report to her). The woman had delegated responsibility for a particular application to one of the men on her team, and the Indian needed to consult with that team member from time to time about the application. Whenever the Indian man had a question about something, he always approached the female manager, who in turn repeatedly explained that she was not involved in that application, didn't know anything about it, and he would have to talk to the male team member who was responsible. Moreover, she told the Indian man he did not have to come to her in the future and that he should go directly to the man in charge. Even so, the Indian man came to her at least twice a week for two months, got the exact same message each time ("You don't need to come to me."), and still kept coming back. After two months of this, the female manager heard that the Indian man was finally going directly to the subordinate on her team without first coming to her.

Advice for Westerners

The solution to the empowerment problem, in all its forms, is for Western managers to make it clear to the Indians they work with that in the United States and northern Europe managers delegate—in fact and not just on paper—that they fully expect and want subordinates to take responsibility for whatever has been delegated to them, and that they do not expect or want to deal with matters they have empowered their subordinates to take care of.

If we apply the six-step coaching model outlined in chapter 3 to this issue, the coaching advice would break down like this:

Step 1. Explain to Indians that you empower your subordinates and want them to take responsibility for the tasks you have delegated to them; they don't need to check with you before taking action, and others don't need to check with you before consulting your subordinates.

Step 2. Explain why: that you consider it inefficient and a poor use of your time when subordinates check with you in these cases and when others ask your permission to consult your subordinates.

Step 3. Reassure Indians that although the empowered behavior you have asked for would be considered usurping the boss's authority in their culture, it is appropriate and expected in yours.

Step 4. Repeat the advice to act empowered a number of times.

Step 5. Give Indians time to practice and get comfortable with being empowered.

Step 6. Give immediate and repeated positive feedback as you see any signs of Indians acting empowered.

Following Instructions—to a Fault

Another management difference that confuses and often frustrates Westerners is the reluctance Indian subordinates appear to have using their own judgment and making independent decisions. In a culture where bosses do not typically empower or delegate, where subordinates are not encouraged to think for themselves, it's understandable that sometimes they do not. "[I]n the Indian culture," Erik Granered writes in his book *Global Call Centers*, "decision-making and general responsibility rest completely with the person in charge. People who are not in charge are reluctant to take on that role because of the heavy burdens that come with it" (Granered 2005, 147).

Those not in charge usually wait for detailed and explicit instructions, and then do exactly as they are told. They are not expected to critique or question the instructions, just to follow them—even when those instructions are incomplete, incorrect, or when subordinates know a better way of doing something. The rationale here is quite simple: if you follow instructions to the letter and do just as you're told—nothing more, nothing less, and nothing *else*—then you can't make a mistake, or, more accurately, you can't be held *accountable* for making a mistake. Rather, the person instructing you would be accountable, providing you did precisely as you were instructed.

This behavior is quite irrational to most Americans and Europeans, not to mention annoying. If it is not entirely what it seems—and it is, in fact, somewhat more complicated, as we will explain shortly—that's still cold comfort to Westerners, who are likely to shake their heads at these behaviors and reach some inaccurate and unfortunate conclusions about the Indians they work with. So let's look more closely at each of these three issues and try to prevent any misinterpretations before they arise.

Incomplete Instructions

For the reasons just cited, many Indian subordinates are hesitant to do anything they have not explicitly been asked or directed to do. Indian subordinates are not comfortable "interpreting" their instructions, going beyond their instructions, or otherwise reaching any independent conclusions about what their boss *might* have meant or *should* have said.

Indian subordinates are not comfortable "interpreting" their instructions or going beyond their instructions.

If, for example, an Indian who has been asked by her boss to fix A and B discovers that C—or even just B.1—also needs fixing, she will probably not be comfortable using her own judgment and going ahead and fixing C. She is much more likely to fix A and B, report this back to her boss, and then mention that C seems to need fixing as well. Or, in some cases, will not even mention C at all since that might embarrass the boss, who should have known that C was also not working and included it in the original instructions.

For the most part, Western bosses are not expecting subordinates to be quite so literal or faithful in their interpretation of instructions.

In low-power distance cultures it is understood that subordinates have a fair amount of latitude in responding to requests or guidance from their boss, since that guidance is usually quite broad and general in the first place, with managers deliberately leaving room for subordinates to use their own judgment. When subordinates do not, this will frustrate a Western manager and may lead the manager to conclude that the subordinate is not very competent, not very confident, or both.

Incidentally, this tendency of Indians not to exceed or stray from their instructions helps explain in part the common complaint many Westerners have when they call a help desk or customer service center with a problem and seem to get nowhere with the Indian on the other end of the line. The Indians in such circumstances have been trained in very precise ways, often with very detailed scripts, to handle the most common problems callers have, and as long as the callers' problems correspond precisely to the scripts, Indians are quite comfortable responding. But if a caller's problem is not quite covered by the Indian's script—if the Indian, in other words, would have to depart from the script and offer advice on a problem for which he or she has not been given *any* instructions—then the individual may become nervous. In many cases, the Indian either tries valiantly to force the caller's problem back into the script (to the everlasting annoyance of most callers) or, failing that, apologizes for not being able to help the caller (and perhaps escalates the call to a higher level). Indians naturally assume that they're doing the right thing in these instances, for in the Indian workplace the consequences of frustrating the customer would never be as serious as the consequences of exceeding one's instructions and quite possibly making a mistake. (It is also generally true that the Indian working environment is not nearly as customer-friendly as the Western one.)

This is the cultural explanation for what may be going on in these help-desk exchanges, but there is often a very practical explanation as well: Indians in customer service positions are often trained in only a few of the most common customer problems and may not know what to say in other cases. Moreover, they may very well have expressly been told by their managers not to give any advice in such cases for fear of telling the customer to do something that might be a serious and costly mistake.

Bad Instructions

More frustrating still for Americans and Europeans is what Indians do when they receive instructions they know are wrong or incorrect. Actually, Indian subordinates usually do one of two things with such instructions: they either accept them without objection and then just ignore them and do what they know is right; or they follow them to the letter and let the chips fall where they may, knowing, incidentally, that one place the chips will *not* fall is on them because in India, as long as subordinates do what they're told, they can't make a mistake.

Indians would usually only follow the first course of action if they were quite confident in their abilities, and in most cases they would neither tell the manager her instructions were wrong (that could be embarrassing) nor that they had ignored her instructions (yet more embarrassment). "They may simply go and do what they consider to be the correct thing," Gitanjali Kolanad has written, "even if it is exactly the opposite of what was ordered, [and] . . . the boss may not even find out that orders were not followed" (2005, 256). While this is not exactly how Westerners would handle this situation, since the task gets done the way it's supposed to—and the looming error is avoided—this behavior doesn't usually bother Westerners, if they even notice it.

The second response, following bad instructions to the letter without saying anything, is another story; this deeply frustrates Western bosses who can't see any rationale for it—and many reasons not to do it. From the Indian point of view, however, there is a certain logic, and it goes like this: the admittedly unfortunate consequences of carrying out bad or inaccurate instructions must always be weighed against the rival set of unfortunate consequences of questioning, challenging—and quite possibly alienating—one's superior, who is, don't forget, also one's benefactor and protector. In many cases, it's no contest; the fallout from questioning or challenging the manager would be much more serious than the fallout from executing a task improperly (at least for the individual, if not for the enterprise). "Everyone . . . just does as they're told," Kolanad continues, "and even if they know the boss is 100 percent wrong, no one will argue. It is difficult to get staff to express opposing views directly—that would be considered discourteous to the boss" (256).

Here Westerners need to remember that in Indian culture questioning a senior person or a superior can be seen as disrespectful and causing offense to one's elder, as well as showing a lack of deference. "Indians are adept at telling you what they think you want to hear," Kolanad has observed. "This is for them a matter of politeness. You must find ways of allowing staff to express opposing viewpoints without going counter to their sense of the boss's absolute authority" (257). Even worse, questioning instructions could cause the boss to lose face, for the implicit message of questioning one's superior—and Indians, don't forget, are experts at decoding implicit messages—is that the boss doesn't know what she is talking about. In cultures where people rely on the favor of the boss to get ahead, subordinates think twice (at a minimum) before making the manager look bad.

> The way Indians question dubious instructions is so polite and oblique—so easy to miss—that most Americans and Europeans do in fact miss it.

All of this notwithstanding, it must also be said that most Indians do not in fact meekly follow foolish instructions and let their managers pick up the pieces. While it *is* a delicate matter to question one's superior in Indian culture, and far more delicate in India than in the West, many Indians will nevertheless challenge guidance they believe to be wrong. The problem for Westerners is that the way Indians question dubious instructions is so polite and oblique—so easy to miss—that most Americans and Europeans do, in fact, miss it. Here are a few examples of the codes Indians often employ to object to bad guidance:

- After getting the instructions, they might casually mention later in the conversation how they once did this same task another way, or even how someone else once did this task another way.
- They will repeat the instructions: "So you would like me to . . . ."
- They will accept the instructions and then, later in the conversation, ask again what the instructions were.
- They may ask if anyone has done this task this way before.
- They may ask if there are any *other* instructions regarding this matter.
- They might ask if they could try something else in case these excellent instructions don't work.

Indian bosses recognize these codes, of course, and hear the objections, but most Westerners do not. For all intents and purposes, while many Indian subordinates do not simply swallow their objections and quietly comply with inaccurate instructions, they might as well as far as most Westerners are concerned. Westerners read this behavior as further proof that Indians apparently don't have the competence, the confidence, or simply the desire to object to poor guidance or bad instructions. Even worse, Westerners could quite reasonably conclude that Indians aren't as concerned about doing a good job as they are about faithfully following instructions.

This perceived Indian reluctance to question or challenge their superiors is especially frustrating for those Western companies—and they are legion—that regard their Indian colleagues not primarily as cheap labor but as expert consultants in a joint undertaking. They value Indian expertise highly and are eager to derive maximum benefit from it, so they are naturally disappointed when Indians appear to be stingy with their expertise. This has become such a common concern that many Indian vendors have taken to warning their employees about it as part of their orientation. "One last point," the orientation manual from one major Indian company reads,

If you know your client is wrong in what they are saying or asking for, find a way to tactfully communicate that to the person immediately. If the situation makes this too uncomfortable, alert your project manager . . . as quickly and accurately as possible as to what occurred. Our clients expect us to be consultants to them, not just programmers. When we agree with everything they say, our role of consultant diminishes.

When Indians Have a Better Idea

Many Westerners have probably had a conversation that went something like this:

> LINDA: Anyway, Anju, I think this is the best way to handle that kind of phone call.
>
> ANJU: I see. You think that will work, then?
>
> LINDA: It should. You remember that's how we did it for the Easter promotion..
>
> ANJU: Yes. I remember. That is how we did it.
>
> LINDA: But if you know another way. . . . .
>
> ANJU: This probably wouldn't work, but one time my group . . . (she describes her idea).
>
> LINDA: Why do you think it wouldn't work?
>
> ANJU: Excuse me?

This conversation actually contains three examples of an Indian doing something many Westerners claim Indians seldom or never do: stating that something the Westerner has proposed would not work and suggesting a better way. Indians prefer to just follow the instructions they're given, this claim holds, even when they know a better way to do something.

There is actually some truth to this allegation but much less than meets the eye. Some Indians, it's true, would be uncomfortable telling their manager they know a better way for fear of acting as if they're more competent than their boss. For one thing, that could make the boss look bad (a nonstarter in face-saving cultures), and for another it might suggest pride on the part of the subordinate. Humility, including false humility, is a very important value in Indian culture, especially for those lower down in the pecking order for whom keeping a low profile is almost always the wisest course. Of course subordinates *do* know better than their bosses in these instances, but it's one thing to know better and quite another to act like it.

What actually happens in cases like these is that most Indians would in fact let their boss know of the better way, but never directly. Rather, Indians will resort to one of their codes, and Westerners, not knowing the codes, once again won't get the message. So what are the codes for this situation?

- Indians will suggest a better way but downplay their suggestion with ritual, entirely *pro forma* disclaimers such as: "This probably won't work but . . . ." This might sound crazy but . . . ." "I don't know if this would work but . . . ."
- Indians will ask if the boss thinks the instructions she has just given is the best way to do the task in question. Note Anju's: "You think that will work then?" Of course Linda thinks it will work; she just said it's the best way to handle that type of phone call. This is not a question, in short, but a polite way for Anju to say she doesn't think much of Linda's idea.
- Indians will conspicuously not say anything positive about what has been suggested, as in Anju's "Yes. I remember. That is how we did it." Absence of positive feedback in this situation is equivalent to negative feedback (See chapter 3).
- Indians will go away and then come back later saying they're having trouble doing the task the way they were told.

Once again the impression left with Westerners, who are not familiar with these techniques, is not very positive: that Indians are too timid to speak up, lack self-confidence, or just don't want to cooperate.

Clearly, our instructions trio of issues is the raw material for a number of serious misreadings of Indians by Westerners. Taken together, these three issues go a long way toward explaining the common Western complaint that Indians don't "take ownership" of their work, think for themselves, or use their own judgment—and do not, therefore, add the value Westerners are looking for when they reach out to Indian partners—all of which can be very frustrating and disappointing for Americans and Europeans. While we can appreciate the logic of these conclusions from the Western point of view, we must remind ourselves again that Indians would be appalled (and also perplexed) to hear themselves characterized in this way.

Advice for Westerners

Fixing the three instructions problems is, once again, partly a matter of Westerners getting better at decoding what Indians are actually saying and partly a matter of coaching Indians to say things in a more Western way. In this particular instance, the coaching would involve three specific behaviors:

- Encouraging Indians to apply instructions, where appropriate, to the entire *category* of things they have been directed to work on and not just the discrete items within the category that were specifically mentioned.
- Encouraging Indians to be more direct (by Western standards) in questioning inaccurate or wrong instructions.
- Encouraging Indians to be more direct about suggesting a better way of doing something.

In each case, the six-step model used above and in chapter 1 can be applied to coaching in these three areas.

Another piece of advice for Westerners concerning the whole guidance and instructions issue is: the more guidance the better. Because Indians are somewhat reluctant to question or interpret their instructions, the more explicit, detailed, and specific they are the happier Indians will be.

While most Westerners prefer general guidance which then leaves them free to exercise their own judgment, experiment, and be creative, Indians can get quite nervous when things are not clearly spelled out. "You really have to give the offshore development teams very specific instructions," observes Joseph Rottman at the University of Missouri at St. Louis, "They really don't show much initiative in going out and investigating a new solution to a problem. When you talk to someone on the supplier [Indian] side, they [often] say, 'The U.S. managers don't give us all the information that we need. They don't direct us. We're kind of left on our own.'" (Overby, 8)

Taking Initiative, Indian-Style

Westerners often perceive Indians as being uncomfortable taking initiative, although most Indians would dispute this characterization. The reason for the confusion here has to do with how each side defines taking initiative. For Westerners, taking initiative means acting on one's own, without specific guidance or direction or the knowledge of one's manager, to solve a problem, improve a process or procedure, or try a new way of doing something. For Indians, initiative would consist of *identifying* these potential enhancements on their own, but it would not extend to taking action without informing their manager. Once again, Westerners who are expecting Indians to be proactive and assume more responsibility for their work—to be full partners and not just hired hands—will probably be disappointed.

The "fix" here is for Westerners to keep emphasizing that, at a minimum, they see their Indian colleagues as their professional equals—or even more experienced than themselves in some cases—and are therefore depending on Indians to be proactive and make substantive contributions wherever they can. Beyond this general advice, Westerners should also give specific examples of what they mean by being proactive and making substantive contributions, citing instances where they expected Indians to offer suggestions or to critique the way Westerners were doing something.

When Indians Don't Understand You

Many Westerners will recognize the following conversation, although it won't necessarily trigger fond memories:

> KATHY: How are you, Dev?
>
> DEV: Great! And you?
>
> KATHY: I'm fine. Hey Dev, on this payroll screen; this isn't exactly what I was looking for.
>
> DEV: I'm very sorry.
>
> KATHY: It's probably my fault, but when I explained this last week and asked you if you understood, you did say yes.
>
> DEV: Oh yes.
>
> KATHY: But I guess you didn't really understand?
>
> DEV: Perhaps not. I did ask Raj, but he couldn't help.
>
> KATHY: No, he's not familiar with this screen. But you could have come back to me.
>
> DEV: Of course.

Another common phenomenon Westerners notice is the apparent unwillingness of Indians to admit when they have not understood something the Westerner has explained to them. This is especially annoying when Westerners find out later—too late, usually—that the Indians had not understood something the Westerners were sure they had, which in turn means that a project is now behind schedule, some work has to be redone, or a lot of time has been lost.

The source of this reluctance, which many Indians will readily admit to, is not hard to find: it's our old friend and nemesis "face." To the Indian way of thinking, when the boss, an expert, anyone senior, or virtually anyone on the client side (whether a boss or not) explains something, it would be disrespectful and a loss of face for the boss if the Indian indicated he or she did not understand because that would mean the boss didn't do a very good job of explaining. Because bosses or experts are supposed to know these things, it's embarrassing if they can't explain them clearly to someone else. All this is especially true, by the way, when explanations are given in a meeting or in front of a group where it would be particularly disrespectful to embarrass the boss. It is also the case that Indians may be reluctant in front of peers, and especially in front of subordinates, to ask too many questions for fear of appearing incompetent.

I was once giving a workshop at NIKE in Portland to a mixed group of Americans and Indians, the latter working on teams led by the former. We were discussing this topic and I turned to the Indians at the table and asked them: "If your boss asks you to do some coding for a particular software application, and you have no idea what he wants, what do you do?" The Indians looked at each other and laughed. "We talk among ourselves," they said, "to see if *any* of us understood." (This is what Dev did in the conversation quoted just above when he asked his friend Raj.) "Fine," I replied. "And what if none of you understood?" "Oh," they answered, "then we just try something and hope it's right." I had given the Indians two chances to give the "right" answer—"We go back and ask our manager for clarification"—and it never occurred to them that that was what the Americans were expecting. It goes without saying that the bosses sitting around the table were not amused.

Western readers probably see an easy fix for this problem: after you explain something to Indians, you do what Kathy does above and just ask them if they understood you. But of course in these circumstances Indians can't really say "no" (as Dev obviously did not) and embarrass you, so a yes/no question to verify understanding is pretty much a nonstarter. Fine, you say; no yes/no questions. So how *do* we find out if Indians have understood us? We really don't want them going off to "try something and hope it's right." How do Indians find out if other Indians have understood them?

Advice for Westerners

Indians also don't want subordinates trying something and hoping it's right. But instead of asking the dead-end did-you-understand question, they use other techniques. One of the most common is to stop after giving an explanation, especially of anything that's new or somewhat complicated, and make it clear that you, the explainer, know this is a bit difficult, you didn't understand it very well the first time either, it takes some getting used to, et cetera, and explain that you know they must have some questions. "So what would you like me to explain again?" In this way the Indians get the clarification and additional explanations they need, but they never have to say they didn't understand because they were never directly asked.

A related technique that Indian bosses often use is not to make a formal offer like this but to go around later to the subordinates' desks and see or ask how things are going. Indeed, in many cases all the boss has to do is show up in the subordinates' work area and they know he has come so they can ask questions. Another technique is to work closely with one member of the team of subordinates until he or she understands and then have that individual take the lead in explaining the task to the other team members. While Indians may be reluctant to tell the boss they didn't understand something, they have no such reluctance with one of their peers.

Another good technique is to ask the team to go off and put in writing what they think you have asked them to do or explain how they are going to do what you have asked, and then show it to you. Indians will often do this without even being asked. In reading what they have laid out, it will be clear that either the Indians have understood and no more explanation is needed, or they have not understood, in which case you can then clear up any confusion. It is important, if you do this, not to come across as doubting the Indians' competence or as being patronizing or condescending. You can avoid this impression by saying that sometimes you're not very clear about what you want or you leave things out, so if they don't mind . . . . Indians will probably know you're just being polite, but your good intentions will be appreciated.

Westerners often say there is another, easier solution to this problem: just ask the Indians to explain back to you what you told them. This often works, but there are two reasons that it may not. One is that sometimes people can repeat the words you used but not really know what you meant, and the other problem with this solution is that when people who have been doing something for years try to explain it to others, they leave out entire steps that they have long since internalized. In the process what is really an eight-step sequence of actions gets reduced to the five steps the speaker can still think of. So the Indian can repeat the five steps the speaker laid out but not the three others the speaker never mentioned.

In addition to doing what Indians do and the other suggestions offered above, Westerners can also coach around this issue. In this case the coaching would involve reassuring Indians that asking questions when they don't understand something is appropriate and expected behavior, that it does not constitute disrespect, and that it does not cause loss of face. "Be prepared to ask clients to explain to you in more detail what they want from you," the orientation manual cited earlier advises,

> if [it is] unclear during the conversation. Usually they much prefer for you to do this versus finding out later that you really did not understand exactly what they were asking you to do. By not asking, your work may fall short of their expectations or you may do something wrong. When either happens, it becomes very obvious to the client that you really did not understand correctly to begin with and that you tried to solve the problem without help from the client.

Subordinates at Meetings

If you've ever led a meeting where your Indian team members or any other Indians you work with, team members or not, were in attendance, then you may have had a conversation like the following (which will be explained in a moment):

BETTY: Ram, hello. Thanks again for your input in the conference call this morning.
RAM: You're welcome.
BETTY: What's up?
RAM: I think I may have some different data from what you presented at the meeting.
BETTY: Oh, I know. I was looking at an old version of the data. I'm just writing an e-mail to everyone. You *knew* that?
RAM: Yes.

BETTY: And you didn't say anything?

RAM: Oh, no.

The behavior of Indian subordinates at meetings is all of a piece with the main points made above. As we have discussed elsewhere in these pages, the sensitivities inherent in the face-saving dynamic are on full display in group settings, such as meetings and conference calls. Simply stated, there are so many faces present at meetings that saving all of them effectively means that not very much can actually be said at an Indian meeting nor, as a consequence, can very much be accomplished. Which is actually the most common observation Westerners make about Indian meetings. The finer points of meetings and conference calls are discussed in chapter 7; here we want only to address meetings in the context of manager-subordinate relations.

The first point to make is that it's actually not all the faces at meetings that need to be protected, just those of the important people, and that would be bosses and any other senior or older figures—as well as anyone from the client organization. The faces of subordinates can actually get quite beaten up at meetings, significantly more so than in the West. Indeed, Westerners are sometimes appalled at the way Indian managers berate their subordinates in front of other people. The second point to make is that the face-saving dynamic is not nearly so operative in meetings of peers. Westerners would not attend such meetings, of course, because if they did it would no longer be a meeting of peers, but if Westerners could observe the meeting of an Indian team, for example, where the team leader was not present, they would see that Indians of the same rank can be very direct, frank, and open with each other.

Indians Won't Correct the Boss

Readers can probably imagine what would happen if an Indian boss misspoke at a meeting and the subordinates at the meeting knew better. Nothing. In Indian culture one does not correct—or challenge, question, or disagree with—the boss in front of others. Not only would that be disrespectful and therefore bad manners, but it would also suggest a lack of humility. Indians will either do what Ram does in this conversation, come around immediately after the meeting to politely point out the mistake ("I think I may have some different data . . . ."), or they might do one of the following during the meeting itself:

- Ask the boss to repeat the incorrect statement (which signals the boss that there's a problem).
- After the boss speaks, refer to the same topic again and give the correct information.
- Bring the conversation back to the topic later, quote the misstatement the boss made, and ask the boss to verify it (giving the boss the chance to discover and correct the mistake).
- Correct the boss privately during a break in the meeting (which are more common than they are in the West, partly for just this reason).
- Whisper a correction to the boss (or hand him a note) when someone else is talking.

Westerners can try coaching Indians in this area—telling them it's fine to correct the manager at a meeting—but it will be an uphill struggle. That behavior is so far beyond the pale for Indians that even if you reassure them it's not seen as disrespectful in the West, Indians may never be comfortable acting in this manner. Even Westerners are somewhat careful about correcting superiors in meetings; the cultural difference here is not so much that Westerners always correct misstatements and Indians never do, but that while Westerners would normally correct minor misstatements (which would not embarrass a typical boss), Indians would be careful even about those.

Subordinates, Not Equals

Another meeting behavior that bothers Westerners is the apparent reluctance of Indian subordinates to act as equal participants at meetings, especially their unwillingness to speak up in front of their managers. The reason, of course, is that they are not equal participants, and they know better than to act as if they were. If a Westerner addresses a question or a remark to a subordinate in a meeting, it's quite common either for the Indian's manager to respond or for the subordinate to turn to his manager to get permission before responding. Indians would never address a question to a subordinate under these circumstances—and if they did, subordinates would not answer—because that would show disrespect for the boss, whose prerogative it is to decide which questions and remarks to respond to and which ones to defer to subordinates. Addressing questions or remarks directly to subordinates, in other words, is likely to be seen by Indians as an attempt to circumvent the chain of command.

Addressing questions or remarks directly to subordinates is likely to be seen by Indians as an attempt to circumvent the chain of command.

Another, closely related cultural norm at work here is the Indian tendency to be quite sensitive to rank, anchored, of course, in the strong sense of hierarchy. Indians are keenly aware of each other's rank, and those of the same rank can interact freely. But if someone of a higher rank wants to interact with someone of a lower rank, which is how Indians would view what happens when Westerners ask Indian subordinates a question, then he should go through someone of equal rank, putting the question, in other words, to the Indian manager.

All this can be very frustrating for Westerners who want to hear from the person who has the information they seek, not the team lead or the person with the highest rank. Indeed, this was so frustrating to the IT folks of one of my clients that they actually asked the Indian team leads *not to attend* the weekly conference call with Poona so the people from the client side could speak directly to the Indian team members who were doing most of the work and who were, therefore, the most familiar with the status of the project and with any glitches there might be. Indians also want to get their information from these same people, incidentally, who are very often subordinates; they're just careful to go through the boss. Once again, Westerners who are unaware of what's going on in these circumstances often reach the wrong conclusion: either that Indian subordinates are timid and not very confident or that Indian managers are defensive, insecure, and arrogant.

The best advice for Westerners here is to surrender. While you can certainly coach the Indians who are *your* subordinates to speak up freely at meetings without getting your permission, if you're in a meeting or on a conference call with an Indian manager and her subordinates, it will be easier on everyone—you, the manager, and especially the subordinates— if you just bite the bullet and direct your remarks and questions to the boss. Another strategy you can try here is to speak to the team leads/ managers ahead of time, explaining that you would like to be able to hear directly from their team members during a meeting, and ask these bosses to tell their subordinates it's OK to talk to the Westerners when they ask questions. Most Indian bosses would be quite amenable to this (and some do it without even being asked).

Subordinates in Training Sessions

A training class is not quite the same as a meeting, but as far as manager-subordinate interactions go, most of the same rules apply. If Indian sub-ordinates are in the same class as their team leader or any other senior people, their instinct, as always, is to keep a very low profile. They will answer if they are called on, as they typically would be by Western train-ers, but they might act hesitant. They will try very hard not to act as if they know more than their boss, although this would be less true with a younger boss who may be their same age. Their superiors, meanwhile, may do most of the talking, not, as Westerners often think, to monopolize the training but only because they know their team members may not say very much. In many cases, Indian managers will make it clear before a training session that they want their subordinates to participate freely and not feel constrained.

Indians, whether they are subordinates or managers, are generally less likely than Western trainees to say they have not understood some-thing, for fear of making the trainer look bad. For this reason, trainers should give more frequent and longer breaks, during which they can expect to be mobbed by Indians with the questions they did not want to ask in front of the whole class and thereby embarrass the trainer. Needless to say, the trainer should be available during the break and not go off somewhere for a coffee or to check e-mail.

We might note in this context that trainees will also be reluctant to give verbal feedback at the end of the session or program about "how the training can be improved." Such feedback implies criticism of the trainers (at least it would to Indians), and Indians will not be comfortable embarrassing the trainers in front of everyone. They would be much more comfortable giving any constructive feedback privately to the trainer.

Praise the Team

Another cultural difference between managers in the East and the West involves giving positive feedback. Indian subordinates tend to regard themselves almost as a family who all work for the same manager. They are much more comfortable acting as a team and sharing responsibility than working on their own, and their preference is to collaborate rather than compete (although they can be very competitive, even cutthroat, vis à vis *other* teams). When an Indian is given an assignment, one of her first instincts is to find someone to partner with, whereas many Westerners would look for a partner only after it became clear the job was too big for one person. Indian subordinates are more apt to speak of "We" than of "I," and they naturally regard their accomplishments more as the product of their combined efforts rather than what any one of them has done individually.

Consequently, Indians are used to being praised and rewarded as a group or team rather than being singled out for individual recognition. Indeed, praising one subordinate in front of the others is not only a slight to the rest of the group but embarrassing to the person singled out. A plant manager at an American manufacturing company once told me the story of his first Indian "Employee of the Year." When he informed Indira that she had been selected, she was somewhat uncomfortable. When he explained further that the award would be given out at an annual employee recognition luncheon, she became quite agitated and asked whether she had to attend. The manager came to understand that Indira was embarrassed because she was singled out in front of her colleagues, and it was agreed that the award would be given to her privately in the manager's office.

This doesn't mean Indians do not like individual recognition in those cases where it is clearly warranted, but from the Indian point of view there would typically be far fewer such cases, and the achievements in question would have to be so obviously personal and individual that one's team members would not feel slighted.

Sir and Madam: Indian Formality

The manager-subordinate relationship is much more formal in India than in the West. Subordinates do not usually call their bosses by their first name (and managers don't usually encourage them to), though this is starting to change. Indian subordinates also tend to use "sir" or "madam" when speaking to the manager, and often stand up when the manager enters the room, enters their workspace, or comes up to engage them in conversation. Finally, some younger Indians may look down and otherwise maintain only minimal eye contact with their elders, as they have been taught to do with parents, grandparents, and teachers at school.

Some Westerners are uncomfortable with this degree of formality and deference and ask Indians to use the manager's first name, to not use "sir" or "madam," and not to stand up in the manager's presence. Most Indians can easily make these adjustments, although using first names will feel too familiar and even impolite to some Indians, especially if the Westerner comes from an older generation than the Indian.

Ingratiating Behavior

Some Westerners are bothered by what they regard as the excessively deferential, subservient, even obsequious behavior of some Indians.

Subservience is simply how you show respect and get ahead in India, but it can easily come across as fawning and insincere to Westerners. "The [manager-subordinate] relationship is . . . latently ingratiating and manipulative," Sinha has written.

> A number of the observers of the Indian scene have reported that flattery is a common social phenomenon in the Indian society . . . .
>
> A supervisor who was ingratiated by his worker positively evaluated the worker in terms of his success, personal promotion, and his potential role in improving interpersonal climate and productivity. The supervisor himself felt more powerful because of the ingratiation by his worker. (1990, 42)

While ingratiating behavior tends to disappear the more exposure Indians have to Westerners, it often shows up in initial contacts. Westerners should simply ignore it.

Young Indian Managers

While the typical Indian manager is certainly more authoritarian—what we have called high-power distance—than the typical Western one, the fact is that there is a growing number of *atypical* managers in the Indian workplace in the person of increasingly young men and women in team leader and first-line supervisory positions. In some cases these Indians are only a year or two older than the people they supervise, or are even the same age. Due to the ever-expanding demand for talent in the offshore boom, Indians who might once have had to work three or four years before becoming a supervisor now find themselves team leaders in a matter of months. These young Indians are new to the workplace, to say nothing of being new to management; before they barely have time to experience work life as a subordinate, they are suddenly given subordinates of their own to look after.

Because of the fact that these Indians are so close in age and experience to the people they supervise and in many cases have not actually
been supervisors for very long, they tend to regard their team members
more as their peers than as underlings, and vice versa. There is, therefore,
much less of the superior/subordinate dynamic in these relationships;
these "bosses" wear their authority very lightly, in other words, and would
be self-conscious and embarrassed if their team acted in a subservient or
deferential manner toward them. So it is that the first boss many young
Indians entering the workforce today encounter is not the traditional
micro-managing authority figure of years past, but a young man or
woman of their same age whose management style, in some respects at
least, may in fact be closer to that of bosses in the West.

These same young people, both the supervisors and their team members, are very often the Indians Westerners end up working with, especially in those situations where Indian companies send some of their staff
offshore to work in the client's workplace for an extended period of time.
Indian firms tend to prefer younger Indians for these positions for a
number of reasons: (1) since they are young, they are more likely either to
be single or married but without children, so it is easier for them to leave
home for an extended stay overseas; (2) young people tend to be more
flexible and adapt more easily to living and working in the West; and
(3) Indian companies want to groom these young professionals for
management positions, and first-hand experience with American and
European client operations is increasingly a key qualification for
advancement.

When these young Indians go to work in the West, they are in some
ways culturally more suited to the management style they find there,
either because they have been managed by other young Indians with a
less authoritarian style, or, even if they were managed by traditional
Indian bosses, they have very often not been in the workplace long
enough for *any* style to have left its mark on them. As might be expected,
these Indians tend to adapt quickly to certain features of the Western
style, although not to all of them, and Westerners, as a consequence, may
find it much easier working with them. These young Indians are used to

being empowered, for example, and may not have any qualms about using their own judgment or acting without first consulting their boss. They may also be used to less guidance and supervision from their immediate supervisors, to being involved in decision-making, and to being consulted for their views and opinions, which they may not be at all reticent to share.

While these Indians are certainly less traditional when it comes to these aspects of the manager-subordinate relationship, against all expectations—and much to the surprise and confusion of Americans and Europeans—they actually tend to be very polite, subservient, and deferential in their dealings *with Westerners*. The same Indians who are not especially subservient where you might reasonably expect it, back in India, are suddenly the picture of deference in the West, where it is not expected!

How does it happen that Indians who treat their young supervisor back home as their peer turn around and treat their Western boss as their superior? One reason is age: while the average age of the Indian first-line supervisor is indeed coming down, the Westerners most of these Indians work with would, at a minimum, be anywhere from five to ten years older than they are. As we have seen repeatedly, deference to and respect for one's elders, regardless of how "elder" they actually are, is a bedrock value in Indian society, and this value kicks in as soon as young Indians are around older people, as, indeed, it does when they deal with older Indian managers in India. In this context we should point out that while an Indian's first-line supervisor or team leader is often one's peer in age and experience, the next layer of management in India would be older, and younger Indians would not regard these individuals as their equals.

Another reason young Indians often treat all Westerners, whether bosses or not, with much more respect and formality is because Westerners are the client, and clients deserve respect and subservience no matter who they are or what culture they come from. Finally, there may still be some vestiges of inadequacy vis à vis foreigners left over from the colonial period when Indians were often treated as inferior by their colonial overlords, and many of them internalized the message. These Indians are no longer in the workforce, of course, but their children are, usually in senior positions by now, and their children's children. While two generations are long enough for the message to have disappeared, it is not necessarily long enough for the subtle feelings of inadequacy it spawned to have entirely died out. "There is still sometimes a sense of insecurity when dealing with the West," notes Paul Davies, who has written quite sensitively about this topic, from a Western point of view, of course

> I've checked this with a good cross-section of my Indian friends, colleagues, and acquaintances. They have agreed that . . . [it] is still a real issue. It has changed even in the years I have been dealing with India, but it is a cross-current of which you should be aware . . . While individual confidence among Indians is rising perceptibly as the years go by, there is a fragility underlying some of it that is revealed in sensitive moments. And the absolute need [for Indians] to be polite will make it very difficult for you to see. . . . (Davies 2005, 134–35)

Whatever the explanation, it turns out that the same young Indians who seem to handle being empowered quite easily still struggle when it comes to acting the equal of their Western bosses. In many situations, they will revert to being very polite and deferential toward Western managers; so that they may be reluctant to speak up when they don't understand something, to challenge bad instructions, to readily suggest a better way of doing something, or to overtly question or correct their boss. They also tend to treat their bosses with what Westerners would consider elaborate courtesy and formality. They are loath, in short, to cause offense, and offense, it must be remembered, can be caused much more easily in harmony-loving, face-saving cultures than in the West.

The lesson in all this for the Westerners who work with these young Indians is to remember that they have a foot in both worlds, yours and theirs, and you can never be sure, in any given situation, which way they are leaning.

Advice for Indians

For our Indian readers, we offer this brief summary of advice for how to work more successfully with Western managers:

- Westerners are expecting you to behave as their equal, not as an inferior.
- It's OK to disagree with a manager, and be sure to do so in what Westerners—not Indians—consider a direct manner.
- Saving face is not such a concern with Western managers, so you can usually be more direct with them and still not embarrass them or be seen as disrespectful.
- Western managers do delegate responsibility and empower their subordinates; you are free—and you are expected—to use your own judgment and make your own decisions regarding those matters that have been delegated to you.
- Do not ask permission to take routine actions.
- Question or challenge (with Western-style directness) any instructions you believe are wrong.
- Do not hesitate to forcefully suggest improvements or a better way of doing something.
- Do not hesitate to ask for clarification if you did not understand something.
- If you work for a Western boss, do not hesitate to speak up at meetings.
- For minor mistakes or errors—the wrong date, the wrong statistic—you can usually correct the boss in front of other people.
- Try not to act overly subservient or deferential with your manager; Western bosses do not like to be treated as superiors.
- Remember: Westerners expect you to act as consultants, not just as cheap labor; they are counting on you to help them improve their products, services, and processes. When you have good ideas, they want to hear them.

General Advice

- Observe closely how Western managers and subordinates interact with each other; this is probably the right way to behave in their culture and, therefore, how they're expecting *you* to behave.
- Don't force yourself to adopt Western behaviors that make you feel very uncomfortable; try to find a compromise between what you would do in India and what Westerners are expecting, something you can live with.

This completes our brief survey of key cultural differences between Indian and Western management. As we have noted above, many Indians reading this chapter, especially younger ones, would strenuously object to some of the characterizations herein, insisting (politely) that it describes a traditional Indian workplace that no longer exists. And they would have a lot of company, for most of the observers of the Indian business scene today agree that the Indian workplace has become increasingly Westernized in the last 20 years, especially companies in the technology and service sectors who have worked extensively with partners or clients in America and Europe.

While there isn't much doubt that the Indian workplace has become less Indian in recent years; whether it has become truly Western is another question altogether. One suspects that even if Mr. Patel, a 60-year-old retired Indian middle manager, would find much that is unfamiliar in today's Indian workplace, it would still be considerably more familiar to him than it would be to the 40-something Mr. Smith from Cleveland. In short, even if many Indians may indeed not recognize themselves in this chapter, a lot of Westerners will swear they've just come from a meeting with Ram, Dev, and Anju.

As further evidence that East is not yet West, I might cite my conversations with a number of young Indians working temporarily in the United States. Almost all of them have told me how much they prefer the American style of management, and while they admitted they had had to adjust in the beginning to the autonomy and freedom conferred on them by their American bosses, they quickly got used to being empowered.

Their only worry now, they confessed, was how they could ever go back and work in India. If these young Indians are so concerned about how they can adjust to working back home, that would seem to suggest that East and West do indeed still manage differently.

Western readers could be forgiven, meanwhile, for wondering which Indians are going to turn up in their workplace: traditional Eastern ones or modern Western ones? Which Indians am I going to have to manage? The best answer, not to be too glib, is to manage the Indians standing in front of you, not some "typical" Indians you read about in a book like this. In fact, some of the Indians you work with will probably be more traditional, some will be more Westernized, and most will be somewhere in between. Welcome to the global workplace.

Best Practices: Management Style

A summary of the main advice to
Westerners given in this chapter

- Encourage Indians to use their own judgment and make their own decisions in areas you have delegated to them; they do not always have to check with you before acting.
- Encourage Indians to approach your subordinates directly about matters you have authorized them to handle; Indians do not have to approach your subordinates through you.
- Encourage Indians to question instructions they think are inaccurate or wrong, and praise them when they do.
- Encourage Indians to speak up if they know a better way to do something.
- Explain to Indians that you regard them as your equals in the relationship, not just hired hands; that you are relying on them to act as expert consultants.
- Explain to Indians that you fully expect them to ask questions if they have not understood you.

- Instead of asking Indians if they have understood you, volunteer additional clarification and see if they accept it.
- Encourage your Indian subordinates to speak up at meetings whenever they have something to say.
- Try to praise the whole team, not just one individual.
- Don't be surprised when younger Indians can be very Western in their behavior one moment and very Indian the next.

Talking Points:
The Language Problem

*Slow down your manner of speech. Your dialect, accent, and pro-
nunciation of words will immediately become more understandable
if you speak more slowly. Our clients repeatedly tell us that we talk
too fast, even after being at the client's site for many weeks.*
Overseas Deputation Manual of a major Indian vendor

While cultural differences between people from India and the West are
complicated and very real, most Europeans and Americans have a much
more immediate problem when they deal with Indians: they don't understand them. Not that they don't understand what Indians *mean* by what
they say (the subject of chapters 2 and 3, on communication style), but
that they don't understand the actual words the Indians are speaking.
Naturally, this comes as something of a shock, not to mention a disappointment; you have been assured your Indian colleagues speak English,
and you do in fact recognize a few words, but the sad truth is Indians can
utter entire sentences—even entire strings of sentences—and you catch
almost nothing of what they're telling you, especially if you're talking on
the telephone. What's going on?

Fast Talkers

First, rest assured: your Indian colleagues are indeed speaking English,
and it is as good as or even better than yours. The problem lies elsewhere,

in three different places to be exact. The first is in the speed with which many Indians speak. India has two main language families: Indo-Aryan in the north and Dravidian in the south. The Dravidian-based languages—such as Tamil, Telugu, Kannada, and Malayalam—are considered the world's fastest languages; that is, in conversation with each other, native speakers of those languages are talking faster than the native speakers of any other language family. And one of these tongues—Tamil, the language of the state of Tamil Nadu (with Chennai or Madras as its capital)—is considered *the* fastest language.

All this becomes important when we realize that the majority of the offshore work is taking place in southern India, from Mumbai south, in such well-known centers as Bangalore and Chennai. So Westerners working with Indians are very likely to be working with southern Indians, those Dravidian speakers who are the world's fastest talkers. The point is that when Dravidian speakers switch to English they tend to speak as fast as they do in their native language, which is too fast for many Americans and Europeans. Even other Indians, especially those from northern India, often ask Dravidian speakers to slow down. We might add here that those Tamil speakers, the language-speed record holders, make up an unusually large percentage—somewhere between 20 and 25 percent—of the Indians working in offshore ventures, especially in the information technology sector.

Indian Accents

But speed alone does not explain why many Westerners can't understand Indians when they speak English. The second factor is accent. Like everyone else, Indians speak with an accent, and it is a different accent depending on what the speaker's first language is. There are 18 official languages in India, roughly corresponding to the states (of which there are actually 28). Most Indians, therefore, grow up speaking the language of their home state. If you grow up in Gujarat, for example, you speak Gujarati; if you grow up in the Punjab, you speak Punjabi; if you grow up in Tamil Nadu, you speak Tamil. When Indians switch to English, they speak it with the accent of their first language. When two Indians meet each other and start speaking English, each one can usually tell where the other is from by that person's English accent. Westerners can't distinguish between these accents, of course; none of these are accents most Europeans and Americans have heard before. Some Indian accents are easier on the Western ear than others, but as luck would have it those tend to be the accents in northern India. Americans, incidentally, are at a special disadvantage when it comes to understanding accented English because, unlike continental Europeans, most Americans don't grow up hearing people speak English as a second language.

Americans are at a special disadvantage when it comes to understanding accented English because they don't grow up hearing people speak English as a second language.

We should mention here that many Indians, especially those who work for customer service or call centers, attend what are known as accent reduction or accent neutralization classes. These classes vary in quality, of course, and results depend on how long one attends and how much of an accent the person had at the beginning, but one thing is common to almost all of these classes: the people who attend them come out with less of an accent than they went in with. While this is expected, of course, and all to the good, such classes sometimes have the unintended effect of misleading Indians who do in fact still speak with an accent, however much it may have been reduced, into thinking they no longer have an accent or have only a very minor one that most Westerners would have no trouble understanding. These Indians, because of such classes, mistakenly believe it's much easier for a Westerner to understand them than it actually is.

We hasten to add, for the record, that many of these classes, especially those that are preparing Indians to work in call centers, are very successful; this is because Indians remain in these classes as long as it takes to minimize their accent, often a period of two to three months. Some Indian companies, although usually not those in the call center business, offer only a two- or three-week "crash" accent program for their staff, and this is normally not enough to be effective.

Indian English

So when you add accent to speed, things get complicated. And they become even more complicated when you consider that by and large Indians aren't speaking American or even British English but Indian English. Indian English is certainly much closer to British than to American English—which gives the British and continental Europeans an advantage in speaking with Indians—but the vocabulary and many of the idioms and expressions are unique to India (and even to certain parts of India). If you don't think so, look at the following list of Indian English words and expressions (none of which are common in the United Kingdom, incidentally) and see how many you understand:

Clubbing	Snaps
Fresher	Hi tech
A cover	A scale
She's eating my brain.	A mixi
Bills	Canteen
Prepone	A real time pass
Good name	Purse
Curd	Homely

(Turn to the end of this chapter for the U.S. and British equivalents.)

The combination of speed, the unusual accents, and unfamiliar vocabulary defeats many Westerners. Those who are not defeated by this mixture give up in the face of a fourth obstacle: the fact that a lot of business is conducted with Indians on the telephone, which means Westerners can't see Indians' body language, such as facial expressions and gestures. Body language, the nonverbal medium of communication, contains much of the message when people speak, and the inability to see

Indian body language in phone conversations forces Westerners to rely exclusively on the spoken words. And the spoken words are the problem.

———————————

The inability to see Indian body language in phone conversations forces Westerners to rely exclusively on the spoken words. And the spoken words are the problem.

———————————

Indians are Caught Off Guard

We should mention that many Indians, in particular those who have not traveled outside India or have had limited contact with people from Europe and the United States, are quite surprised to learn that Westerners have trouble understanding them, and they may not initially believe this. This is because they have been speaking English all their lives and no one has ever accused them of speaking with an accent or using unfamiliar vocabulary— no one, in short, has ever had trouble understanding them *before*. The problem, of course, is that they have been speaking English to other Indians who speak exactly the way they do, and they have therefore come to regard this way of speaking as standard English, as opposed to what it actually is: standard *Indian* English. It is only when they speak to someone outside of India, therefore, someone who has not grown up hearing Indian English, that Indians discover they talk with an accent and use unfamiliar vocabulary. (This is true of anyone who has a regional accent, of course, such as an Englishman from Yorkshire or an American from the South; when they go outside their region or speak to someone from another region, they too are surprised to learn they "talk funny.")

The point is that many Indians have a very good reason (i.e., their life experience to date) to wrongly assume that it is easier for Westerners to understand them than is actually the case. Initially, then, they are quite likely to forget that Westerners aren't used to Indian English (speed, accent, and vocabulary) and likewise forget to adjust their English for the Western ear. Meanwhile, Westerners, who may have indicated to their Indian colleagues how hard it is to understand them, may be frustrated when Indians don't seem to be modifying their speech. Indians are not trying to be difficult in these instances; they're just having trouble remembering who they're talking to!

Don't Interrupt Me

Although it is not really a language problem per se, another frustration for Westerners is the tendency for some Indians to interrupt them before they have finished speaking. In the United States and northern Europe (but generally not southern Europe), speakers practice what is known as turn-taking, which effectively means that speaker B does not begin to speak until speaker A is finished, signaled by a pause of two to three seconds. When speaker A pauses, in other words, it is speaker B's turn to speak. So the exchange looks something like what is shown in Figure 6.1.

Figure 6.1 Western turn-taking.

In India it is acceptable and therefore not uncommon for speaker B to begin speaking before speaker A has finished, especially if it is clear to B what speaker A is trying to say. The result is some "overlap" at the end of A's turn and the beginning of B's, and the exchange looks like this

Figure 6.2 Indian turn-taking.

To Westerners the Indian overlap feels like and actually is an interruption and is considered rude. This issue has become common enough that a number of Indian companies routinely caution their employees about it in their orientation literature. *Do not interrupt* when your client is in mid-sentence," a pamphlet from one vendor warns:

> Our clients tell us that too often we attempt to answer questions before they are fully asked, many times answering something that is not actually what the client is trying to ask of us. [Wait] until you completely understand what the person is asking or until the person has stopped talking . . . even if you think you already know the answer. Americans will tolerate this a time or two but eventually become irritated when someone consistently does this . . . . (manual cited earlier)

The confusion around turn-taking may be the source of a common Western complaint that Indians tend to monopolize the conversation, never allowing Westerners to get a word in edgewise. This phenomenon may actually be Indians waiting for Westerners to interrupt them in the customary places (customary for Indians, that is), and when Westerners do not—because to interrupt is rude—the Indian assumes the Westerner has nothing to say and keeps on talking.

Some observers have noted that the Indian overlap pattern means that Indians tend never to put anything important at the beginning of their remarks because the other person isn't yet listening; they tend, rather, to begin with ritual comments and then, when the other speaker has finished and is in fact paying attention, to move on to the substance of their message. Westerners, by contrast, tend to put the important points right up front and for this reason often mistake Indian ritual remarks for real substance, paying attention in effect, to the wrong part of the conversation.

Advice for Westerners

So what's a Westerner to do? To begin with: relax. It takes time, but it's possible to get used to speedy Indians and to any accent, Indian accents included. With repeated exposure to how Indians speak, Westerners get better and better at understanding them. For this reason, Westerners should orchestrate as much exposure to Indian speech as possible, talking with—or better yet listening to—Indians every chance they get, in spite of the initial frustration. While you may have to rely on e-mail for important matters, seek out the Indians in your workplace to chat with about non-critical topics, join them for lunch, speak with them on social occasions at work, or invite them out after work. If the only Indians you deal with are offshore, then consider calling them whenever possible instead of or in addition to sending them e-mails. You can also rent English-language Indian films. All this will take a lot of patience in the beginning, but there is no substitute for this kind of exposure to Indian speech.

You should also not hesitate to ask Indians to slow down, repeat, or rephrase if you have not understood them. Southern Indians are quite used to this, incidentally, as even northern Indians ask them to slow down. But even if they aren't used to this, most Indians learn sooner or later that Westerners sometimes have trouble with Indian accents.

Another strategy is to follow up a conversation you didn't completely understand with an e-mail in which you summarize what you think was said, and ask for confirmation. Or you can ask Indians to put in writing what they have said. In both instances, it's important to try not to make the Indians feel bad for causing you so much trouble (which they will anyway). You can explain that you're "not very good with accents," that it's sometimes hard to catch everything over the telephone, or that you "just want to double check to be sure."

Another approach that sometimes works is for Indians to select the member of their group or team (or among those attending a meeting) who has the least accent to do most of the talking. Sometimes Indians will offer to do this on their own, or you can try to find a diplomatic way of suggesting they do so. One cultural obstacle here (see chapter 5) is that managers usually do all the talking at meetings and during all important conversations with Westerners, while subordinates keep a very low profile. But the manager may not always be the Indian with the least accent.

Video-conferencing offers at least the possibility of seeing some of the Indian nonverbal communication, which, as we have noted elsewhere, carries much more of the meaning of a conversation than it typically does for Westerners.

Sometimes nothing works. The Indian slows down, repeats, and tries all the other tricks he knows to get through to a hapless Westerner, and the Westerner still doesn't understand. In these cases practically the only thing the Westerner can do is to ask the Indian to write down what he's saying. If the conversation takes place on the phone, this request will sound fairly harmless. If you're worried about making the Indian feel bad, you can just say you'd like a written copy for your files. If it's a face-to-face conversation, you can just ask the Indian to send you an e-mail when he gets back to his desk because you like to keep a record of these things!

One thing Westerners should watch out for is finishing Indians' sentences for them in cases where Indians appear to be struggling to make themselves understood. This is not usually a problem because Indians don't typically struggle this way, but when they do the instinct for many native English speakers is to help the other person by supplying the words they seem to be searching for. While Westerners are trying to be kind, the message this often sends to non-native English speakers is that this conversation is taking too long, which only makes the person speaking nervous and self-conscious.

Meanwhile, Watch Your Own Speech

The language problem goes both ways, of course. While Westerners usually don't speak as fast as Indians, they too speak with accents and use vocabulary, idioms, and colloquial expressions Indians don't always understand. People from the United Kingdom and Europe have to worry less about this than Americans because they tend to speak British English, which is closer to Indian English, and they also tend to speak with British accents, which most Indians are familiar with.

Westerners also speak with accents and use vocabulary, idioms, and colloquial expressions Indians don't always understand.

Even so, all Westerners need to be careful of their speech and be willing to slow down and especially to avoid colloquialisms and idiomatic expressions, such as those listed here. There are hundreds of these, incidentally, but this list will give readers a general idea of the phenomenon. (Indian readers should turn to the end of this chapter for translations of these expressions.)

It's up in the air.
We'll just have to wing it.
That's a piece of cake.
They're getting cold feet.
We're out on a limb.
That's a real can of worms.
He doesn't have a prayer.
She's under the weather.
They bit off more than they could chew.
No sweat.
That will never fly.
Give me a ballpark figure.
It's a whole new ballgame.
We struck out.
That was a close call.
He's out in left field.
He hit it out of the park.
That was a home run.
You'll never get to first base with that idea.
They threw us a curve (or curve ball).

Americans should be particularly careful about using baseball expressions.

Some young Indians working in Boston once told me how surprised they were the first time they went to the "restroom" to find toilets but no couches or easy chairs.

Westerners should also ask Indian colleagues at the end of a conversation or before moving on to a new topic in a conversation if there is anything the Westerner needs to repeat.

Remember: Indians Won't Ask You What You Mean

Westerners would not have to be quite so careful about their speech if they could trust Indians to tell them when they have not understood something the Westerner has said. But Indians will not usually do this. Indians, especially younger ones, don't want to be a nuisance, to cause frustration, or to take any more of the Westerner's time than necessary (or in some cases to admit they don't know a particular expression); so when a Westerner says something an Indian doesn't understand, the Indian will usually not say anything and either guess at what the Westerner meant or, after the Westerner leaves or hangs up the phone, ask other Indians who were present if they understood what the Westerner was saying.

The tendency for Indians not to ask Westerners for clarification of a point complicates the speaking dynamic considerably because it means Westerners have to self-monitor their own speech and catch themselves in the act of phrasing things in ways Indians may not understand—and then rephrase what they have said. Most people are not in the habit of monitoring their speech in this way, so this is a skill that has to be consciously worked on.

All this is somewhat easier in face-to-face conversations. If you unknowingly use a colloquialism or idiom an Indian does not understand, you may be able to tell from the confused look on his face, which becomes your cue that you need to rephrase. Needless to say, these confused looks— hence, the cues—are not available to you in a phone conversation or e-mail, where the burden falls completely on you to monitor your speech more closely. Here again video conferencing can sometimes be helpful, provided you can clearly see the faces of the Indians you're talking to.

The fact that many Indians are reluctant to tell you when they have not understood you argues again to not hesitate to ask Indians to slow down, repeat, or rephrase when you have not understood them. The more often you do this to them, the more comfortable they will feel doing it to you.

Advice for Indians

Here are a few quick tips for how Indians can make their conversations with their Western colleagues go more smoothly:

- Slow down.
- Don't assume your accent has disappeared just because you attended an accent reduction class for a week or two; it may have been reduced but usually a week is not enough to eliminate an accent.
- Remember that Westerners may be embarrassed to ask you to slow down or repeat something; just because they do not ask this does *not* mean they have understood you. Look for signs that they may be confused.
- If Westerners use expressions you do not understand, be sure to ask them what those expressions mean.
- Be careful of using Indian English vocabulary and expressions that Westerners may never have heard before.
- Remember that it is much harder for Westerners to understand you on the telephone than in person, so be especially careful to slow down.
- Be careful not to interrupt Westerners, to start speaking before they have completely stopped.

Here is the meaning of the list of Indian English expressions on page 128.

Clubbing (combining)	Snaps (snapshots, photos)
Fresher (novice, someone who just started)	Hi tech (modern, up to date)
A cover (an envelope)	A scale (a ruler)
She's eating my brain. (giving me a hard time)	A mixi (a blender)

Bills (receipts or invoices)

Canteen (cafeteria)

Prepone (move forward, opposite of postpone)

A real time pass (waste of time)

Good name (a polite way to ask someone their name)

Purse (wallet)

Curd (yogurt)

Homely (a good home-maker/ housewife)

Here is the meaning of the mainly American idioms on page 134.

It's up in the air. (It has not been decided.)

We'll just have to wing it. (We just have to try it and see what happens; we don't have a plan.)

That's a piece of cake. (That's very easy.)

They're getting cold feet. (They have some concerns; they're getting nervous or worried.)

We're out on a limb. (We're taking a chance or taking a risk.)

That's a real can of worms. (That's a lot of problems, a real mess.)

He doesn't have a prayer. (There is no chance or possibility.)

She's under the weather. (She's not feeling well.)

They bit off more than they could chew. (They are trying to do more than they can handle.)

No sweat. (That's not a problem.)

That will never fly. (That won't work.)

Give me a ballpark figure. (An estimate, a rough guess.) ⎫

It's a whole new ballgame. (A new set of circumstances a new situation.) ⎪

We struck out. (We failed.) ⎬ American baseball expressions translated

That was a close call. (We almost made a mistake.) ⎪

He's out in left field. (He's not aware of what's going on.) ⎭

He hit it out of the park. (He did a very good job.)

That was a home run. (That was very successful.) .

You'll never get to first base with that idea. (That won't work.)

They threw us a curve. (They did something we were not expecting.)

Best Practices: Talking Points

A summary of the main advice to
Westerners given in this chapter

- Be patient; you may think you will never understand Indians or a certain Indian (they talk too fast or you don't understand their accent). You *will* get used to their way of speaking the more you hear it.
- Don't hesitate to ask Indians to slow down.
- Don't hesitate to ask Indians to repeat something you didn't understand.
- To get used to an Indian accent sooner, rent English-language Indian movies.
- It's harder to understand Indians on the telephone than face to face (when you can see their facial expressions and body language).
- It's easier to understand Indians on a video conference call than on an audio-only conference call because you can see their body language.
- Don't be offended if Indians start speaking before you have stopped; this is not rude in their culture.
- If you're worried that you did not understand something an Indian said, send an e-mail summarizing what you understood and ask the Indian to verify.
- If you can't understand something an Indian is saying, ask him to put it in an e-mail and send it to you.
- Be careful of your own speech; try not to use colloquial expressions (It's up in the air. That's a piece of cake) which Indians may not be familiar with. They won't ask you to explain these things; they will just try to guess what you mean.

Meetings and Conference Calls

Let's cover the parts of meetings [in India] that will be familiar to an American, a Belgian, or a Brit:

It will probably start.
Time will elapse.
You will end the meeting.

Paul Davies
What's This India Business?

Most Westerners who have attended an Indian meeting have the same reaction: "That was a meeting?" The purpose and to a large extent the conduct of Indian meetings are so different from what Westerners are used to that they don't always recognize an Indian meeting even when they're attending one.

Meetings

Let's start with the purpose. In the United States and northern Europe, a meeting is essentially the coming together of interested and involved parties to jointly discuss the various matters on the agenda and, ideally, to make decisions regarding them. (The exception would be information meetings where the purpose is for managers to inform subordinates of important developments and decisions made at higher levels.) In an effective meeting, everyone is an equal participant, regardless of his or her place in the pecking order, and all attendees are expected to freely expresses their opinions or views on the matters under discussion, which results in a great deal of what Americans call give and take. Participants are permitted—even expected—to disagree with one another, to question one another, to challenge each other, and generally to not be afraid to air their differences. These differences are then discussed and ultimately reconciled as far as possible, at which point a consensus emerges and a decision is made that is agreeable to at least a majority of those present (often obtained by a vote of all the attendees). At the end of the best meetings, participants leave with "action items," things they can now go off and do as a result of decisions made during the meeting. All this is not what actually *happens* at every meeting, of course, but it is certainly the ideal.

A typical Indian would not be caught dead at such an event (and if he were caught at such an event, he would probably *wish* he were dead). For reasons discussed earlier about the collective and hierarchical nature of Indian society, most of the things that occur at a typical meeting in the United States and northern Europe would not be possible at an Indian meeting. Of the behaviors mentioned in the above paragraph, for example, the following would not be common in a typical Indian meeting:

- All attendees act as equal participants regardless of rank.
- Views are expressed freely.
- Give and take occurs.
- Differences are aired.

Looking at this list, a Westerner would immediately wonder how Indians get anything done at a meeting. And the answer, not surprisingly, is that they don't. Getting things done, as commonly defined by Westerners, anyway, is simply not the purpose of an Indian meeting or, therefore, the measure of a good one.

So Why Meet?

While it is not necessary for a Westerner to completely understand the logic of an Indian-style meeting in order to meet successfully with Indians, it helps to know where Indians are coming from in order to: (1) realize how Indians perceive certain norms of Western meetings, and (2) to either adjust one's own meeting behaviors to suit the Indian style or coach and mentor Indians to adjust their behaviors to suit the Western style. Or both.

So, if getting things done is not the purpose of an Indian meeting, then what is? We should note that Indians actually do get things done at meetings, very important things, in fact; they're just not things Westerners consider important. And most of the things Westerners *do* consider important would be difficult to accomplish at the typical Indian meeting.

To understand Indian meetings remember that the overriding concerns are to avoid confrontation, to allow all parties to save face, and to not offend anybody.

To understand Indian meetings we have to once again remember that like almost all other encounters between people in Indian society the overriding concerns are to avoid confrontation, to allow all parties (including oneself) to save face, and to not offend anybody. This makes any kind of group event, such as a meeting, problematic because the more people involved in an encounter, the more faces there are to worry about. Practically speaking, this concern with face severely limits what can be said in front of other people and therefore what can be said at a meeting. In the final analysis, any limits on what can be *said* at a meeting are bound to limit what can be *accomplished* at a meeting, because meetings are basically nothing but talk.

Here is a partial list of things that could conceivably cause loss of face and/or offense and which, therefore, cannot normally be done at a meeting or at the very least would have to be done very carefully:

- Disagreeing with what someone else says, especially if he is senior.
- Correcting what someone else, especially a senior, has said.
- Criticizing someone else who is present.
- Challenging something another person says.
- Making an overtly negative comment about what someone else has said.
- Giving negative feedback.
- Saying something is not possible.
- Admitting a mistake.
- Admitting that you do not or did not understand something.
- Admitting that you are not on schedule, are falling behind, and are not going to make a deadline.
- Asking for help or for more time.

These are common and necessary tasks in any workplace, of course, and they are no less common or necessary in India than anywhere else; they are just not normally done in public. Rather, these delicate tasks are conducted in private, one-on-one conversations before the meeting or, sometimes, in smaller, breakout meetings of subgroups where the risk of causing disharmony and losing face or causing others to lose face are minimized.

Indians meet not so much to discuss and deliberate but to present the results of their discussions and deliberations.

Once a Westerner understands this, a lot of things about Indian meetings begin to make sense, starting with the purpose. The objective of most Indian meetings is not so much to reach agreement and make decisions; it is, rather, to announce decisions after participants have reached agreement through numerous one-on-one discussions. Indians meet, in short, not to discuss and deliberate but to present the results of all the discussions and deliberations that have preceded the meeting. Indian meetings actually resemble quite closely the last few minutes of the typical

Western meeting, when participants have reached agreement and are no longer discussing substantive matters.

How Indians Conduct Meetings

The conduct of Indian meetings is all of a piece with this purpose. Agreements are described and decisions announced, and the only discussion is usually about any details that still have to be worked out. Indians are quite comfortable discussing details in public, often ad infinitum, because they are less sensitive and less important and therefore not particularly contentious. Disagreements about details usually do not threaten harmony the way disagreements about substance can.

Another common element of Indian meetings is to announce upcoming issues that will need to be discussed and agreed upon by those present before the next meeting. In most cases, preliminary discussion of these issues will begin at this point, allowing participants to see where everyone stands or how everyone feels about the issues. This discussion reveals where there are likely disagreements and differences of opinion, thereby indicating which participants will need to talk to each other one on one and reach agreement before the group can move forward and make a decision. If no differences of opinion emerge at this stage, then the issue can in fact be decided at the same meeting where it is introduced.

For these reasons, a common occurrence in Indian meetings is for the discussion to be proceeding along nicely (from the Western perspective) when suddenly the topic is dropped and participants take up another issue, leaving the previous one unresolved. The conversation might sound like this:

> MARK: So, Vinod, I guess we're all ready to design that inventory interface.
> VINOD: Actually I wanted to call you about that after the meeting.
> MARK: Now's a good time to discuss it, while everyone's here.
> VINOD: I think we may have a few questions.

MARK: No problem. Fire away.

VINOD: We *are* ready to get started on the claims screen.

This sort of thing usually happens when Indians sense that meeting participants are far apart on an issue (what Vinod means when he says "I think we may have a few questions") and that there will have to be one-on-one conversations to bring the two sides together (which is why Vinod wants to call Mark back *after* the conference call). Sometimes these conversations take place during breaks, after which the dropped issue is once more on the table and agreement is quickly reached. For this reason, Indian meetings tend to have more breaks and last longer than American and European meetings. Western participants should make sure they are available during breaks. This also explains why meeting by conference call is frustrating to Indians because that type of meeting doesn't usually have any breaks.

Another common technique for handling contentious issues is for the large meeting to break into subgroups where there can be more give and take without so much risk of causing offense. Westerners, as Paul Davies describes, are often surprised when these sub-meetings begin by bringing up for discussion items that were already agreed on in the larger meeting. "I have too often left the main meeting in India," he writes, "to create a small subset of those involved—a favorite Indian approach—and found that we haven't even got to what I regard as the first stage, despite the main meeting having so far been characterized by what I took to be violent agreement, centered on the word yes" (Davies 2005, 130). These sub-meetings often culminate in the various small groups getting back together to announce the results of their deliberations.

The Role of Subordinates

The behavior of subordinates at meetings has been discussed at some length in chapter 5, as it is heavily influenced by the manager-subordinate relationship. Suffice it to say here that Westerners may at times be frustrated by the seeming reluctance of subordinates to participate as equals in meetings, or even, on occasion, to answer questions put directly to them. Traditionally, subordinates defer to their bosses in most public settings, and meetings are no exception. Subordinates are also reluctant to correct misstatements made by their superiors during meetings for fear of embarrassing them. This is another reason to take at least one short break during a meeting so subordinates can correct their manager in private. We will offer some suggestions below about what Westerners can do to increase participation from subordinates during meetings and conference calls.

Conference Calls

Many Americans and Europeans "meet" with their offshore colleagues via regular conference calls. These are still meetings, of course, albeit not of the face-to-face variety, and they are subject to all the considerations described above. But they also have a number of other features that can further complicate the meeting dynamic. For one thing, conference calls almost never include breaks, and breaks offer Indians important opportunities to conduct one-on-one discussions on delicate topics, to air and resolve differences of opinion in relative privacy.

Another problem with conference calls is that they don't allow meeting participants to see each other's body language, which can be a serious challenge for Indians. As we noted in chapter 6, when Indians have something difficult or delicate to communicate, they often confine the real message to nonverbal communication—gestures and facial expressions—and then verbally express what the other person wants to hear or what allows everyone to save face. This allows Indians the comforting and often necessary possibility of saying one thing (what they have to say) while communicating another (the real message). Indians may tell you they can execute a certain task by a certain date, for example, but demonstrate considerable discomfort in their body language (a furrowed brow, a nervous laugh, squirming in their seat), thus indicating their real position on your request. But if you take away the nonverbal option, this forces Indians either to be much more direct in their speech, which will be very uncomfortable for them, or to say what they have to say and then be obliged to follow up with a one-on-one phone call or with an e-mail to communicate what they would otherwise have "said" in their body language.

Another drawback of conference calls is that Americans and Europeans can't see the faces of their Indian colleagues and thus do not have any way of knowing when they have said something the Indians don't understand. As we noted in chapter 6 on language, when Indians don't recognize an idiom or an expression, if the Westerner is talking too fast or with a strong accent, or if the Indian simply doesn't understand what the Westerner means—in these cases Indians are reluctant to ask for clarification, especially in front of other people. But when Westerners can see the Indian they're talking to, they may notice the frown, the knitted brow, or the baffled expression on that person's face and thereby realize they have confused him. And when the Westerner sees this look, she is prompted to clear up any misunderstanding. But when the Westerner cannot see the facial expressions, as is the norm in most conference calls, there is no prompting, and therefore no clarification. And the Indian is left to guess what the Westerner meant—and may guess wrong.

Advice for Westerners

There are a number of implications for Westerners who lead meetings with their Indian colleagues. While Indians would not normally expect Westerners to run meetings the way Indians do, there are some fairly simple things Westerners can do before, during, and after a meeting to make the experience more comfortable for their Indian colleagues, and therefore more effective for both parties.

Before the Meeting

As noted above, it will be much easier for Indians if they can discuss difficult or delicate issues with Westerners one-on-one ahead of time. So they will want to know ahead of time what issues are going to be discussed at the meeting and what the position and wishes of the Westerners are on these topics. This is why Indians try to announce the topics of the next meeting at the current one, so they can gauge initial reactions and identify the people they will need to talk to to begin forging a consensus.

This also means Westerners should be careful not to spring anything on Indians during a meeting, bringing up a topic that has not been announced previously. Or, if Westerners do have to bring up a new topic, then they should not insist on a resolution if there is clearly not general agreement. In this same vein, if in preliminary, one-on-one conversations, it becomes obvious that the parties are still quite far apart on an issue, Westerners should be willing either to postpone the meeting or to set aside the contentious issue until a later meeting.

If Westerners need to talk to or hear from a subordinate at a meeting, it usually works better if the subordinate and her boss know this ahead of time. The boss can then speak to the subordinate and explain that it's OK for her to discuss this issue if Westerners ask her about it. Subordinates are not reluctant to speak up if they know it's OK with their manager.

During the Meeting

It would be easier for Indians if Westerners could keep in mind the following suggestions:

- Don't bring up matters that have not been raised prior to the meeting (except for details, minor issues, or if you already know there is general agreement on the topic).
- If you sense hesitation, don't press the issue.
- Be careful about asking subordinates to speak unless you have set this up ahead of time, and back off if you sense they are uncomfortable.
- Address your comments and questions to bosses (and let them pass these on to their subordinates if they are so inclined).
- If you have to say anything critical, preface it with lots of praise.
- Try to speak more slowly and be careful of idioms and expressions.
- Let Indians take a break if they want to or ask them if they'd like a short break. (This is tricky during a conference call, of course, but it

can still be done, especially if it is positioned ahead of time as a regular feature of every conference call.)

➤ Stick around during any breaks (in face-to-face meetings); the Indians often call breaks explicitly so they can talk to you one-on-one about a delicate issue.

➤ Agree to any suggestion for a breakout meeting of one or more sub-groups where difficult issues can be discussed in relative privacy.

Many Westerners have observed that some Indians try to talk "over" them during meetings, interrupting them and even raising their voice to cut off the Westerner. While this seems impolite to Americans and northern Europeans, this is actually quite common in Indian conversations and is not regarded as rude (see the section in chapter 6 on turn-taking). The one- or two-second time lag in some conference calls also means that one participant may not realize that another participant has already started talking, with the result that both parties are talking over each other. Indians will usually not be offended if you persist in these instances, even by raising your voice in order to claim the floor.

Whatever happens at a meeting, remember above all else to keep your cool; people who get upset in front of others embarrass themselves as well as the other meeting participants.

After the Meeting

The single most important thing to do after a meeting or conference call with Indians is . . . nothing at all! Because it can be difficult for Indians to give bad or disappointing news—such as admitting to delays, mistakes, problems, or to not understanding something you have explained to them—or to otherwise say anything that might embarrass themselves or others, "the truth" is often a necessary casualty of Indian meetings. Indians will save difficult observations or topics for after the meeting, for a phone call, for example, or a one-on-one, face-to face encounter, or, even more common, for an e-mail. For this reason, Westerners should wait a few hours before acting on anything Indians have said during a meeting to give Indians time to follow up with additional or "revised" remarks that may differ somewhat from what they had to say during the meeting. "A real Indian meeting," Davies writes, "starts to conclude and wind down with a series of agreements. Pay no attention. These are agreed at the meeting. Even if they are written down at the time or subsequently, these actions will be the subject of reinterpretation" (Davies, 137).

Westerners should wait a few hours before acting on anything Indians have said during a meeting to give Indians time to follow up with additional or "revised" remarks.

Another best practice post-meeting is to send a follow-up e-mail to your Indian colleagues (after waiting for theirs, of course) summarizing your understanding of what the Indians told you. If you're worried that you may have misinterpreted an Indian who was perhaps being polite or shading the painful truth, then write him or her describing what you believe the individual said during the meeting and ask the Indian to verify your understanding. If you have in fact misinterpreted the Indian, and he sees that you have misunderstood him when he reads what you've written, the Indian won't just let you go on with your mistaken impressions. He or she will write back to clarify any misunderstandings.

Similarly, if you're worried that an Indian has not understood something you said and did not want to embarrass you or take too much of your time by asking a lot of questions, call the Indian back (or send an e-mail) after the meeting and ask whether there is anything he/she would like to talk more about or anything the Indian would like you to clarify. This allows Indians to get their questions answered without ever having to ask any!

Advice for Indians

A few practical suggestions to make meetings easier for your Western colleagues are

- It's harder to offend Westerners than Indians, so don't worry about disagreeing with them, critiquing something they say, or offering an opinion different from theirs; they expect this.
- Westerners often ask questions directly of subordinates; if you're uncomfortable answering in front of your boss, discuss this with him/her ahead of time and get permission to respond to the Westerner.
- Don't agree with something at a meeting and then call the Westerner later to disagree; try to express disagreements *at the meeting*.
- If you do not understand something a Westerner has explained at a meeting, ask for clarification *at the meeting* (not later in a phone call or e-mail).
- If Westerners use idioms or expressions you do not understand, ask them what they mean.

Best Practices: Meetings and Conference Calls

A summary of the main advice to
Westerners given in this chapter

- Be sure to allow Indians to take a break if they want during a meeting.
- If Indians do call a break, be sure to stay in the room so they can talk to you.
- If Indians want to break up the larger meeting and form subgroups for smaller meetings, let them.
- If you want to hear from a subordinate at a meeting, try to let his or her boss know this ahead of time.
- Try not to use idioms and colloquial expressions that Indians may not understand.
- Be careful about giving negative feedback or criticizing someone's idea in front of others.
- If Indians suddenly drop a particular subject during a meeting, don't try to bring it up again.
- If Indians seem hesitant to discuss a certain topic, don't insist.
- Don't bring up subjects that Indians are not expecting you to talk about (unless you know they agree with you on the subject).

- Never act right away on anything you hear at a meeting; always wait for a few hours to see if Indians call or e-mail you with "revised" information.
- If you're not sure you have understood what Indians told you at a meeting, send them an e-mail explaining what you think they said and ask them to verify your understanding.

Women and Men

*[Priya] is the first woman in her family to go to college, and recently
told her parents that while they are free to arrange her marriage,
they must pick a man who will not interfere with her career.*

Business Week
August 22, 2005

The comments about Priya quoted here capture perfectly the evolving status
and role of women in India. Priya belongs to a transitional generation of
middle-class Indian women who can be typically Indian one moment—she
will let her parents arrange her marriage—and perfectly modern the next:
she went to college and is firmly focused on her career. Though women like
Priya have been around for some time in the Indian upper classes, what is
new is their growing presence in the middle class, and especially in the workplace where women now comprise close to one-third of the labor force.

As the status of women has evolved in India, so too has the nature of
their relationship with Indian men, who are never quite sure which Priya
is going to show up for work each morning. Safe generalizations about
the subservient and deferential behavior of women toward Indian men,
especially in public, and the correspondingly condescending attitude of
Indian men toward women, are no longer safe. That is not to say that
these generalizations are now officially false, only that they are no longer
adequate to describe the increasingly wide range of Indian attitudes and

behaviors regarding gender. While it is not necessary for Westerners to understand all the nuances of the evolving male-female dynamic in India—Indians themselves are just beginning to come to terms with it—it can help if they are aware of the general direction in which Indian society is moving and any consequences for people in the West who work with Indian men and women. Needless to say in India, as in most countries, there are vast differences in social attitudes between urban and rural areas and between more educated and less educated people. The observations about men and women in this chapter apply mainly to urban, educated Indians of the middle class.

Traditional Gender Differences

Traditionally, the sexes were much more segregated in Indian society than in the West.

Traditionally, the sexes were much more segregated in Indian society than in the West. In the traditional Indian home, girls and young women were not regularly exposed to men who were not their relatives or close family friends. Girls and young women did not have nearly as much freedom as boys and young men of the same age, especially outside the home where unmarried women rarely ventured without male escorts or in groups of older women. Even today many rural and traditional women will pull the upper part of their sari over their face if they encounter a man they do not know.

When girls started elementary school, they were usually escorted by an older brother or some other male relative, and boys and girls went to separate schools. Most schools are mixed today, but boys and girls typically sit in separate sections of the classroom, especially when they get older and enter secondary school. Even when they grew up and married, men and women traditionally tended to socialize with their own gender much more than in the West.

For women who worked outside the home, who were the exception, the separation of the sexes continued; they either worked in all-female settings or in mixed settings where the women were segregated from the men as much as possible and had minimal interaction with them. The exception to this practice was the government sector; in the Indian civil service, it has always been more common to find men and women working together.

Traditional Hindu teaching stressed the subordination of women to men, Pratap Bhanu Mehta has observed (in his essay "Hinduism and Modernity")

> and all kinds of practices that secured this subordination—child marriage, secluded widowhood, preference for a male child— were enforced in the name of religion.
>
> What is equally striking is that [the] . . . reform movement dislodged the ideological legitimacy of the subordination of women. Formally the Indian state . . . has been extremely progressive and even the last vestiges of discrimination are being removed. But the reality of women's lives remains one of appalling subordination.

Girls were raised to be subservient to men—to defer to them, to obey them, and to wait on them. Very young girls and girls in their early teens also had many more household responsibilities and duties than men: washing and ironing, cleaning the house, preparing for and cleaning up after meals, looking after younger brothers, and doing anything else their elders asked. For their part, boys and young teenage men were typically spoiled by their mothers and aunties, especially the first-born son. Antics that would earn young girls a serious reprimand would earn boys little more than a quick frown. In many families, especially poorer ones, only boys were sent to school. Even today, illiteracy is nearly twice as high among girls as among boys, with 78 percent of girls dropping out of school versus 48 percent for boys (Kripalani 2005, 95). Childhood ended early for a young girl, almost before it began, while it stretched into the mid-teens for a young man. In this context we might note, as many Western women have, that Indian men are much less likely than Western men to defer to women, by permitting them to go first into a building, a room, or an elevator, for example, or by holding a door open for a woman.

This traditional picture has changed a great deal for today's younger Indians, of course, especially in urban areas among more educated, affluent Indians, but in many ways the differences are more of degree than of kind. There is less segregation of the sexes, especially in southern India where women seem to enjoy more equality and interact more freely with men, but there is still much more segregation than in the West. There are also more women in the workplace, especially in the sectors involved in the offshore boom. Boys and young men are probably not as indulged as they once were, but even less traditional Indian parents tend to place more of their expectations, hence more of their attention, on their sons than their daughters.

Writing recently in *The New York Times Magazine*, Chandra Prasad describes the dynamic, foot-in-both-worlds dimension of life for today's female professionals, illustrating why gender is such a moving target for would-be cultural pundits. "Even among my pretty female cousins," she writes,

> bright and lovely Neet stood out . . . [A]t 23 she was sheltered in ways that I, born and bred in the U.S., had trouble comprehending. Neet never left the house alone; she had never even shopped for her own saris. But she had studied rigorously, earned a master's degree in computer science and was working as a software development intern, When I asked her by phone if I'd have to start calling her "Dr. Neet" soon —a nod to the possibility of a doctorate—she laughed and said, in her tentative English, "I like the sound of that!"
>
> In truth, further educational aspirations were at odds with Neet's circumstances, and when I learned last year that her parents were considering arranged-marriage options, I felt sorry for her. (Prasad 2007, 74)

Gender in the Indian Workplace

Vestiges of traditional gender differences linger on and help explain certain male/female interactions in the Indian workplace. For one thing, some Indian men, especially middle-aged men, may not have had much experience working with women as their counterparts. They may find it awkward to work closely with a woman on a team, for example, and prefer to relate to and work primarily with the other male team members. Several young Indian women have told me stories of how male members of teams these women worked on regularly made key decisions as a group and then "informed" the female team members.

Many Indian women often have to assert themselves much more than their male counterparts to get the same attention and respect that men get as a matter of course.

Needless to say, this behavior causes women to become isolated and makes it difficult for them to function as full and equal members of the team. In some cases it also works against women getting interesting and challenging assignments, the kind they need to develop professionally and advance their careers. Indeed, many Indian women often have to assert themselves much more than their male counterparts to get the same attention and respect that men get as a matter of course. This explains in part why Indian women who succeed in the workplace are often much more outspoken and generally "tougher" than men in comparable positions. But even these women, it should be pointed out, will sometimes be quite submissive around Indian men, especially older men, although generally not around Western men.

Female Managers

The gender dynamic gets considerably more complicated when Indian men work for Indian female managers. It goes without saying that Indian men who find it hard to accept female team members as equals have an even harder time reporting to a female boss. This is still not common in the Indian workplace, but where it does occur it can be difficult and awkward for the men involved, although it is generally *not* that difficult for the women, who know what to expect and have long since learned how to handle male subordinates. Indian men may not be used to being given orders by or having to defer to women, although in most cases the deeply hierarchical nature of Indian culture means that the manager-subordinate dynamic overrides the gender dynamic here, with the result that most Indian men are quite subservient to their boss, regardless of gender. Many Indian men would not ordinarily expect a female boss to command the same degree of respect, to be consulted and listened to by her superiors, as a male manager in the same position and would probably, if given the choice, prefer to work for a male manager. It should not be surprising that female Indian bosses tend to be extremely self-confident and have very strong personalities.

No discussion of the gender issue as it plays out in India would be complete without addressing the Indira Gandhi "problem." The first thing many Indians, especially men, will say if a Westerner asks about the status of women in India is that India was the first country to have a female prime minister, at which point your interlocutor may permit himself a smug smile. To begin with, the statement is not true—Sri Lanka actually had the first female prime minister in the person of Mrs. Bhandarnaike—and beyond that it is misleading and just a little disingenuous. India did indeed have a woman prime minister, but the relevant point is not that Mrs. Gandhi was a woman but that she was the daughter and only child of India's first prime minister, Jawahar Lal Nehru. If Mr. Nehru had also had a son, one suspects that he—and not his sister—would have become prime minister.

Indian Women and Westerners

The typical Indian woman in a professional work environment has endured a lot to get to where she is and is generally as competent and confident as any of her male counterparts—and often more so. If the woman in question is working with Westerners in any kind of offshore venture, then she has probably been more carefully selected for this responsibility than many men would be. These facts explain in part the observation by some Americans and Europeans that the Indian women they deal with in the West tend to be more outspoken and direct than their male counterparts (especially if the women are in supervisory positions).

At the same time, many Westerners often find that some Indian women defer to Indian men in meetings and other group situations, especially if they are in the same jobs as the men. In these situations, such as conference calls and meetings, Westerners may be surprised that the Indian men do all the talking, regardless of their competence or familiarity with the topic, even answering questions the Westerners put directly to the Indian female team members. Later, when the Indian men are no longer around, Westerners are often taken aback to find these same soft-spoken, deferential women are every bit the professional equals of their male colleagues men. This phenomenon can be quite frustrating if the Indian woman in the meeting is the one who is most familiar with the topic under discussion or the one who has the solution to the problem at hand.

Westerners can do one of two things if they find themselves in this situation: they can talk to the woman later when the Indian men are no longer around, or they can coach all the Indians involved about how Western-style meetings are conducted, with each person at the meeting expected to participate as the equal of all the others and no one keeping their views to themselves until a more convenient time. While the former approach may offer quicker results, the latter makes more sense for the long term.

Western Women and Indian Men

Westerners, women in particular, are usually more concerned about dealing with Indian men than with Indian women, especially Western female managers. While the potential is certainly there for cultural problems in this regard, they seem to occur far less often than Westerners expect, and generally involve Indian men not relating well to Western female team colleagues (as opposed to bosses). As noted above, some middle-aged Indian men may not have been exposed to that many female counterparts or managers in the Indian workplace, or, if they were exposed to women, they tended to keep their distance and not interact with them as equals. These same men, out of habit, may initially react to Western women the same way; that is, they may be somewhat awkward and uncomfortable around them and may be protective toward them. In the worst cases (worst for Western women, that is), Indian men may fall back on their habit of not regarding women as full partners of the team and therefore be less inclined to consult with them or include them in making decisions.

Western women on the receiving end of this treatment are well advised to educate their Indian colleagues on the gender realities of the Western workplace. In truth, they should not have to work very hard at this piece of cultural coaching, for any Indian man who is even minimally observant will soon notice how Western men interact with Western women—and take the hint. It is worth pointing out, however, that some of the subtler types of gender bias elude even *Western* men, to say nothing of Eastern ones.

[W]hat matters to an Indian . . . is not that the boss is a woman but that she's the boss. And all Indians know how to behave around bosses.

The biggest concern of many Western women is that Indian males will not know how to cope with a Western female boss. While women managers are indeed considerably rarer in India than in America and Europe, the expected cultural problem does not materialize here because of the hierarchical nature of Indian society. Indians may indeed be surprised to have a female manager, but what matters to an Indian in this situation is not that the boss is a woman but that she's the boss. And all Indians know how to behave around bosses.

Speaking of Western women managers working in India, Gitanjali Kolanad has observed that they

> had no trouble establishing their authority. In fact they said they never had to. It was simply accepted. Two women said they actually had many more problems in their home country . . . . What it comes down to is that the boss is the boss, whether male or female. The Indian subordinate accepts that a woman in a position of responsibility must be good at what she does; otherwise she wouldn't be doing it. (2005, 257)

Most observers agree that Indian men have more difficulty adjusting to an Indian female boss than to a Western one.

Young Urban Indians

A lot of young urban Indians would object to some of the characterizations made earlier. Indeed, in conversations with young Indians, I have encountered two very distinct schools of thought on the topic of whether men and women enjoy equal opportunity and receive equal treatment and respect in today's workplace. Many Indians, both men *and* women, say that significant gender differences no longer exist in the workplace, while others, especially Indian women (whose stories are woven into the preceding text), insist that they do.

Both camps do agree on one point: if there are any differences, they are much less evident in the information technology and business process outsourcing sectors, where by some estimates women occupy from one-quarter to one-third of all positions. This assertion is credible, given that these two sectors of the Indian economy are effectively brand new, less than 20 years old, and have repeatedly had to go where Indian society has never gone before.

In the end, since even the experts—young Indian women professionals—are somewhat divided on the subject of gender, we are left with the sage advice we have given elsewhere in these pages: Westerners will have to make their own observations and reach their own conclusions.

Working with Indians on Virtual Teams

Many Indians and Westerners are going to encounter the cultural differences described in this book while working together "virtually," rather than face to face. They are not going to spend a great deal of time (if any) in each other's company, are not going to know each other very well, and they are not going to enjoy close personal relationships. That's unfortunate, because people who know each other well readily forgive the other party all manner of eccentricities and faux pas. Close relationships, in other words, can survive a great deal of misunderstanding, cultural and otherwise, because the parties involved have considerable reserves of trust and goodwill to fall back on. Weaker relationships, such as virtual ones, buckle more quickly under the strain of cultural misunderstandings and collapse that much sooner when the going gets tough. This makes raising the cultural awareness of East-West partners an even greater priority for virtual teams.

> Weaker relationships, such as virtual ones, buckle more quickly under the strain of cultural misunderstandings and collapse that much sooner when the going gets tough.

The team dimension of virtual teams actually comes naturally to collectivist, group-oriented Indians, much more naturally than it does to most Westerners (who typically have to attend team-building workshops to learn how to behave in groups)! Indeed, working in teams with one's colleagues at work feels more or less like an extension of the family dynamic Indians are used to at home. The virtual dimension of virtual teams, on the other hand, is hard on Indians, who do not readily extend their trust to people they don't know well—to people they seldom or never meet, in other words, such as their fellow virtual team members.

A Matter of Trust

Most observers agree that trust is in fact the glue that holds successful teams together, whether virtual or not, and they likewise agree trust is typically the first casualty of most virtual teams. In this chapter we will look at how Indians and Westerners on virtual teams can build more trust and better prepare themselves for the inevitable onslaught of culture.

What makes one member of a team trust the others? In most cases it is one or more of the following factors:

1. We know the person from extensive interaction.
2. The person is technically competent.
3. The person is reliable; he or she follows through and does what they say they are going to do.
4. The person gives you honest feedback (including correcting you when you're mistaken).
5. The person admits mistakes.
6. The person admits when he or she doesn't know or understand something.
7. The person is not afraid or too proud to ask for help.

Recalling a number of the cultural observations made elsewhere in these pages, we will briefly examine these seven factors, indicate where and how culture complicates each factor on an Indian-Western virtual team and then offer suggestions for overcoming these complications.

We Know the Person from Extensive Interaction

While group-oriented Indians trust completely the other members of their collective, including the collectives they form at work, this trust comes only after considerable interaction with group members, much more interaction than Westerners typically require before extending their trust. Therefore, the fact that members of virtual teams have limited interaction—and almost no face-to-face interaction—makes it especially hard for Indians to develop trust on a virtual team. Accordingly, Indians and Westerners should identify and take advantage of every opportunity to meet face to face and spend time in each other's company. Time and costs permitting, here are some suggestions to maximize face-to-face meetings between East-West team members:

- Try to arrange kick-off events when a team first forms and allow plenty of time for unscheduled social interaction.
- Arrange for regular (annual, semi-annual) follow-up meetings.
- When new members join an existing team, if possible they should have preference the next time someone has to travel.
- When team members travel to the site(s) of other team members, make sure they meet as many of the other team members as possible—and not only the people they are specifically traveling to meet with.
- Rotate which team members travel so that as many different members as possible get to meet their teammates.
- If a team member travels to only one site in a country where there are team members located at other sites, try to bring the members from these other sites to that location (or send the traveler to those other sites to meet these other teammates).
- If time and costs preclude meetings of the entire team, identify opportunities for 3-, 4-, or 5-person meetings.

Since the opportunities for real interaction may be limited, team members should also identify and pursue opportunities for virtual interacting, such as those suggested below:

- Hold more virtual meetings and make sure everyone attends, or it defeats the purpose. (Keep meetings short if team members complain about too many meetings.)
- Make sure people identify themselves when they talk during a conference call (so members get to know the personalities).
- Use video-conferencing (rather than conference calls) for meetings if possible.
- Encourage team members to contact each other by telephone—not e-mail—as much as possible. If a team member is typing an e-mail to an Indian or Western colleague, she should ask herself if the colleague is at his desk at this moment; if he is, the team member should call.
- Create a Web site or bulletin board where you post pictures and personal information about team members.

The Person Is Technically Competent

Certain typical cultural behaviors tend to cast doubt on Indian technical competence in the eyes of their Western colleagues.

As we have suggested elsewhere (chapter 5), certain typical cultural behaviors tend to cast doubt on Indian technical competence in the eyes of their Western colleagues. The tendency to always check with their bosses before acting, to hesitate when answering questions at a meeting, the perception that Indians blindly follow instructions even when they know a better way or that the instructions are wrong, the perceived reluctance to challenge or question authority figures—to the Western eye all these behaviors (what we have summed up as the "deference syndrome") make Indians come across as unsure of themselves and lacking in technical ability. This leads directly to charges like "Indians just want to be told what to do" or "Indians don't like to do the thinking part," which are direct quotations from an English manager at HSBC. When people work together in the same location, they can quickly get a sense of each other's technical competence through first-hand observation, but when all they have to go on are occasional phone calls and e-mails—the spoken and/or written word—the evidence is necessarily vague and inconclusive, and the circumstances are thus ripe for misinterpretation, especially if the parties are from different cultures.

The best fix for this problem, once again, is to create opportunities early on in a team's life for members to spend time in each other's company. Another fix is to create a Web site where the credentials and prior experience of all team members are posted. A third suggestion is to educate all team members in the common cultural differences that result in the kind of misreadings described above. Wherever culture is thought to be part of the "problem," then cultural training should be a candidate for the solution.

The Person Is Reliable: They Follow Through and Do What They Say They Are Going to Do

The perception of reliability is an early and common casualty in many Indian-Western interactions, largely because of the differences in communication style we examined in chapters 2 and 3. Westerners mistakenly believe Indians have promised something when they have not, and when Indians do not deliver on these "promises," trust immediately starts to break down. Indians and Westerners on virtual teams need to resolve the classic communication problems discussed in chapter 3 as soon as possible, following the advice offered in that chapter. Perhaps the most relevant piece of advice in that chapter on the whole reliability issue is for Westerners to check in more frequently with Indians to see how work is progressing and to listen closely to what the Indians are actually promising. A good rule of thumb here is never to ask closed (Yes/No) questions, such as "Are you on schedule?" but open questions such as "Where are we on the schedule?" or "Can you show me how much work you still have left to do?"

The Person Gives You Honest Feedback (Including Correcting You When You're Mistaken)

Honest feedback, if it is negative, is practically an oxymoron in Indian culture. Indians do give negative feedback, as we have noted in chapter 3, but when they do they use language and formulas most Westerners do not recognize, with the result that Westerners accuse Indians of not being honest with them. At this point, trust takes yet another hit, and our East-West virtual team continues its downward spiral. The best advice here, once again, is for team members to educate themselves in the different ways of giving honest feedback in their respective cultures so that each side correctly interprets the feedback from the other side. We have also recommended (in chapter 3) that Westerners coach Indians in this regard and that Westerners seek out more one-on-one encounters with Indians where it is more comfortable for Indians to be "blunt."

The Person Admits Mistakes

Among peers Indians are usually quite honest about admitting mistakes, at least among their Indian peers, provided—and this is a major proviso—there is no loss of face involved. With other team members, then, Indians will admit mistakes, but team leaders would typically not be comfortable admitting mistakes in front of their team at a meeting or during a conference call, for example, and members of one team would probably be reluctant to admit mistakes in front of other teams (with whom Indians can be quite competitive). Wherever the client is involved, however, the dynamic is much more sensitive; admitting mistakes to the client, including team members from the client side, risks loss of face and is not easy for many Indians.

The best way for Westerners to handle the whole "mistakes" issue is to focus on correcting the problem and not worry about identifying the guilty party. With most mistakes, after all, identifying who is to blame is much less important than figuring out how the mistake happened and how to prevent it in the future. In those cases where it is necessary to finger the perpetrator, doing so with maximum discretion and minimum public exposure will go a long way toward protecting the individual's face. In such cases it is almost always preferable (where feasible) to turn the "investigation" over to Indians who will know best how to proceed. Two other strategies for Westerners here are (1) to model the behavior they're looking for by being quite open about admitting their own mistakes and (2) to seek out one-on-one exchanges where Indians, especially superiors, may be more comfortable admitting mistakes.

The Person Admits When She Doesn't Know or Understand Something/The Person Is Not Afraid or Too Proud to Ask for Help

These last two factors are closely related, and both also touch on the issue of saving face. Once again, among their peers Indians are normally quite comfortable admitting they don't know or don't understand something and asking for help, but superiors (e.g., team leaders) would typically be embarrassed to do these things in front of subordinates or with people from the client organization. We have also pointed out elsewhere that some Indians are uncomfortable admitting they did not understand something a senior explained for fear it would make the senior look bad. Naturally, Westerners might very well construe the apparent reluctance of Indians to engage in these behaviors as excessive pride or attempts to hide something or be misleading, and this would certainly undermine their trust in Indian team members. The fix here is some cultural awareness about the importance of saving face and about the ways Indians do manifest these behaviors (chapter 3), some coaching for Indian team members, and use of more one-on-one conversations. Once again, if Westerners can also model these behaviors themselves, then that may create a climate which emboldens Indians to be more forthcoming (Western-style) in these areas.

Clearly, cultural differences in communication style and management style complicate the ease and speed with which East-West teams can develop trust. It is axiomatic that almost nothing erodes trust more quickly than misunderstanding and misinterpretation, and the potential for both is automatically present in almost all cross-cultural interactions.

In concluding this section on trust, we summarize the key strategies for Westerners that we have described or implied in the preceding discussion:

- Arrange as many opportunities as possible for team members to spend time face to face.
- Increase each side's awareness of key cultural differences to minimize the chances for misinterpretation.
- Be careful to model the behaviors you are expecting from your Indian counterparts.
- Seek out one-on-one conversations, where it is more comfortable for Indians to say "difficult" things.
- Coach Indians about Western expectations in these key areas.
- Be more proactive about offering help, guidance, additional explanations, and more time so that Indians don't have to ask for these things.

The Timeliness Factor

Another factor that complicates matters on East-West virtual teams is the problem of time zones, which is especially acute for Americans but also a problem for northern Europeans. Because Mumbai or Bangalore is 12.5 hours ahead of California, 9.5 ahead of New York, and 4.5 ahead of London, it is often very difficult to communicate in real time with India. As a result, when an issue comes up in India or in a Western country requiring consultation with the other side, there's a good chance it cannot be resolved the same day. This is frustrating enough, but it's also true that issues often cannot be resolved by direct discussion, such as via telephone or instant messaging. Instead, these issues have to be addressed and resolved through sequential e-mails that do not permit a real-time exchange of information and ideas, of proposal and counterproposal, for example, or suggestion and reaction. As anyone who has been a part of such "discussions" will attest, they can be very protracted, time-consuming, and frustrating. When the issues involved are urgent, which they usually are, and everything is on hold until there is a resolution, the seemingly glacial pace of these exchanges can be maddening.

When an issue comes up in India or in a Western country requiring consultation with the other side, there's a good chance it cannot be resolved the same day.

Most global teams have solved this problem by selecting one or two days a week when key people agree either to stay late or come in early, so they are available during more of each other's work day. In some cases it also helps if key team members exchange their their cell and/or home phone numbers so that in emergencies they can get in touch with each other before the person has come in or after they've gone home.

Learn the Hierarchy

We've made the point in numerous places in this book that the Indian work environment—indeed, all of Indian culture—is very hierarchical. In the case of virtual teams, it is not always easy for Westerners to know the hierarchy, who reports to whom, who is older than whom, or who is looked up and deferred to for some other reason such as caste, social background, or family status. This is important in Indian culture, as we noted in chapter 4, because it is the senior, older, and respected members of the team who are the gatekeepers, the people to whom most queries should be put, whether in a conference call or an e-mail, or at least through whom they should be routed. Making requests or asking questions of the wrong person either results in getting no answer or the answer being delayed while the wrong person consults with the right one. Knowing the chain of command saves a lot of time.

Virtual teams are a challenge under the best of circumstances, and multicultural virtual teams just add another layer of complexity to an already complex dynamic. Such teams can and do work, but they typically take longer to get up and running, and team members will need a lot of patience in the beginning. Meanwhile, they can help themselves considerably by learning as much as possible about the culture of their fellow team members.

Business and Social Etiquette

What strikes me the most upon the whole is the total difference of manners between them and us, from the greatest object to the least. There is not the smallest similitude in the twenty-four hours. It is obvious in every trifle.

Horace Walpole
Letters

In addition to the many beneath-the-surface cultural differences that have been our focus in these pages, there is another dimension of culture, usually called do's and don'ts, that Indians and Westerners who work together often ask about. These differences normally do not lead to the serious cultural problems we have described in earlier chapters, the misunderstandings and misinterpretations that can undermine smooth working relations, but they can cause confusion and embarrassment. While Indians and Westerners both tend to forgive each other the common transgressions and faux pas associated with business and social etiquette, they can still be the source of some anxiety for the foreigner. It is also true that you will make a better impression if you are aware of and respect these cultural norms.

It is important not to confuse a knowledge of do's and don'ts with understanding or being effective in a foreign culture.

At the same time it is important not to confuse a knowledge of do's and don'ts with understanding or being effective in a foreign culture. These are mere details, and while getting them wrong can be a nuisance, getting them right only gets you so far; it's a little like knowing which is the salad plate and dessert fork at a dinner party but not knowing where the dining room is. In other words, if you've turned to this chapter first, hoping to find a shortcut to understanding Indians (or Westerners), you're out of luck— there is no shortcut.

TOPIC	U. S. A. & NORTHERN EUROPE	INDIA
Greetings	A handshake. Embracing is common with close friends of either gender (to show affection) but not with strangers.	Traditionally Indians greet with the *namaste* gesture (for Hindus): palms joined at chest level, fingers making a steeple, often accompanied by a slight nod. But the handshake is now very common. Women would not typically shake hands with men; Western women should wait for Indian men to extend their hands. Embracing is also OK with friends, to show affection, but is only done with someone of the same gender.
Names	The given name comes first, followed by the family name. North Americans and the British tend to address people by their first name; Germans are less likely to do so. North Americans do not use "sir" or "ma'am" with a boss.	Some regional variety but increasingly Indians give their given name first, followed by their family name. Indians tend to use first names with their age peers, last names with all others. Sometimes a last name (Rajakumar) will get

Names (cont'd)		shortened (Raja or Raj) and used as a first name. Indians will often use "sir" or "ma'am" with a superior.
Titles	No. Americans and the British use titles less often (and a person's title and level of education do not usually appear on a business card). Germans use titles more often and often indicate title and level of education on their cards.	Titles are important and commonly used. One's title and university degree(s) often appear on a business card.
Dress	A jacket and tie are more common in Europe than in the United States, but you may have to take off the tie in some settings. Women wear a dress, or a nice skirt and blouse, or a pants suit. The U.S. is more informal in some areas (especially the west coast) and in some sectors (IT, for example, but not banking or the financial sector). Dress in the south and northeast of the U.S. tends to be more formal.	A jacket and tie are always safe for men but often not needed, especially in the south where it is much warmer. A dress or long skirt is safe for women; women should keep their shoulders and knees covered. A hat is often a good idea to protect against the sun.
Eating	North Americans entertain at home; Europeans will invite you to a restaurant. It is not common to wash your hands before or after a meal (but you can if you wish). Keep your elbows off the table. When people go out for lunch from work, each one usually pays for her own food. Most Westerners eat most foods; some Jewish people don't eat pork and some Westerners are vegetarian. It is acceptable to take something from your plate and put it on	Indians are more likely to entertain in their home than in a restaurant. Do not touch food with the left hand but it is OK to pass dishes with the left hand. Do not offer food from your plate to someone else or take food from his plate. Don't drink from someone else's glass. Don't touch food in a common plate with your hand or your utensil.

(Continued)

TOPIC	U. S. A. & NORTHERN EUROPE	INDIA
Eating (cont'd)	another person's plate for him to taste. You can take a sip from another person's glass.	Indians usually wash their hands before and after a meal and rinse out their mouths. Muslims don't eat pork and Hindus don't eat beef; many Indians are vegetarian.
Drinking	Most Westerners drink wine and alcohol, but not all, so it's best to ask.	Muslims and Sikhs are not supposed to drink, but many do. There are probably as many Indians who drink as those who do not. Indians will always offer alcoholic and non-alcoholic beverages.
Shoes	Worn in almost all places, including churches. Westerners will not expect you to remove your shoes when entering their home or apartment.	Not usually worn inside the home, never worn in temples or mosques.
Gifts	If you're invited to a North American's or European's home as a guest, appropriate gifts are: flowers, chocolates, nice biscuits (called cookies in the United States), wine, or a nice Indian handicraft. Westerners will expect you to open a gift when they give it to you, and will open yours upon receipt.	If you're invited to an Indian's home for a meal, appropriate gifts are: a box of sweets or pastries, fruit, or flowers. Indians usually do not open a gift when they receive it or in the presence of the giver. Gifts are not normally wrapped in white paper (which is the color of mourning).
Smoking	Increasingly banned in public places and in the workplace in the United States, somewhat more common in Europe. Always ask before smoking in someone's home.	More common than in the West, in public places and even in the workplace. Always ask before lighting up.

Tipping	People tip in restaurants (15 to 20 percent of the bill in the United States), taxi drivers (around 10 percent of the fare), luggage handlers such as porters (at least $1 per bag, depending on distance). In Europe a service charge may be added to the restaurant bill, in which case tipping is optional.	100 rupees is a common tip for a taxi driver or a luggage porter. 10 percent is a common tip in a restaurant.
Public Displays of Affection	Physical contact between men and women in public— holding hands, embracing, kissing—is appropriate.	Physical contact between men and women in public is not appropriate. Men may hold hands/ walk arm in arm with men and women with women; this has no sexual overtones.
Personal Space	North Americans and northern Europeans usually stand 18 to 24 inches apart in conversation.	Indians stand somewhat closer than Westerners.
Pointing	North Americans point with the index finger; northern Europeans point with the head or with the whole hand.	Some Indians point with the chin; pointing with one finger is normally considered rude.
Eye Contact	North Americans maintain eye contact at least 50 percent of the time when they are listening to someone else; for Europeans it is usually a higher percentage (except the English, who maintain less than North Americans). It is considered impolite not to look the other person in the eye when they are talking to you; it means you are not paying attention or not interested.	Many Indians feel it is impolite to look the speaker in the eye if the person is older or in a senior position. This is less common among young Indians.
Touching	No taboo areas.	Many Indians feel you should not touch people

(Continued)

TOPIC	U. S. A. & NORTHERN EUROPE	INDIA
Touching (cont'd)		on the top of the head, although this can be done as an act of blessing.
The Feet	No special taboos.	Indians try not to sit with the sole of their foot (considered unclean) pointing at another person. They also try not to sleep with their feet pointed toward anyone's head or to step over another person.
The Left Hand	No special taboos.	Considered unclean; avoid using whenever possible. Try not to touch food with the left hand.
Personal Questions	Only with close friends. It's generally not polite to ask if someone is married or has children or how much something costs.	OK to ask if married (Why not?), do you have children (Why not?), how much something costs.
Attitude Toward Time	Westerners don't feel they have enough time; they schedule themselves very tightly (in 10- and 15-minute intervals); it's rude to be late—and late means anything more than 5 minutes. Deadlines are sacrosanct; if they have to be changed or somehow "adjusted," you must advise Westerners in advance. Missing a deadline, even by a day, is a serious matter.	Generally Indians are less obsessed with time and more forgiving if someone is late. (The traffic in Bangalore or Mumbai does not respect anyone's appointment book.) It's not a problem to have to reschedule a meeting or appointment. Deadlines are a loose approximation rather than a firm promise; so many things can happen that are outside anyone's control, there's no point relying too heavily on a deadline. Generally Indians in the West understand the Western preoccupation with time and try to adopt a more obsessive approach.

Caste in India

Many Westerners want to know what role caste will play in their interactions with Indians. The answer, as anyone who has worked with Indians will tell you, it depends on which Indian you ask. Some Indians, especially younger, urbanized types, will insist that caste is no longer very important in Indian culture, at least not for their generation. Many others, including some of those same young, urban types, will swear that caste is still very important and affects many aspects of daily life. The consensus seems to be that while caste is not as great an influence in Indian life as it once was, it has hardly disappeared.

"Caste continues to raise its ugly head again and again in modern India," Gitanjali Kolanad has written:

> It still determines who gets ahead and who does not for the majority of Indians. Most Hindus would find it difficult to imagine a casteless social system. A glance at the matrimonial page of the newspaper is enough to confirm that. Even the ancient association of caste with colour remains, and everyone wants a fair-skinned bride. . . . (2005, 63)

Almost everyone agrees that whatever part caste plays in contemporary Indian life, Westerners are not likely to notice it.

At the same time, almost everyone agrees that whatever part caste plays in contemporary Indian life, Westerners are not likely to notice it. Since most Westerners don't understand how caste works, they wouldn't be able to see caste even if they were looking right at it, which they often are.

This is not the same as saying that Westerners are not affected by caste, because they can be. Not in the sense that caste norms and restrictions would be applied to them—they are, in fact, outside the caste system ("outcasts," which is where the word comes from)—but in the sense that by not understanding caste, Westerners are likely to find certain caste-driven Indian behaviors either incomprehensible or attribute them wrongly to some other cause. Westerners might wonder, for example, why a certain Indian is selected or promoted when another is obviously more qualified, why certain team members always make the coffee while others do not, or why some Indians help move the copying machine as others stand idly by. In India, these could all be caste-related behaviors, but a Westerner would not know this and might find other, less charitable explanations for these actions.

In closing we remind the reader again that respecting the do's and don'ts of another society, important as that is, is not a substitute for the hard work of learning about the values and world view of people from a different country and how these influence their behavior. That's no doubt disappointing for those in search of a quick fix to cultural problems, but then quick fixes are notoriously unreliable.

Epilogue

Now it is not good for the Christian's health to hustle the Aryan brown,
For the Christian riles and the Aryan smiles and he weareth the Christian down.
And the end of the fight is a tombstone white with the name of the late deceased,
And the epitaph drear: "A fool lies here who tried to hustle the East."
—Rudyard Kipling
"The Ballad of East and West"

American and European readers who have reached this point in our text could certainly be forgiven for wondering why companies in the West would ever want to partner with Indians. And our Indian readers might likewise wonder what they're getting themselves into when they sign up to work with people from Los Angeles or London. Who needs all these headaches? But if we've focused in these pages on the things that go wrong when Indians and Westerners work together, which we obviously have, that's not because things usually *do* go wrong, but only because it's when things don't work out that people need the kind of help offered here.

Don't Forget the Good News

So we hasten to add in these closing pages that it's not all headaches and stress when West meets East; many things, in fact, go quite well. Indians and Westerners learn to understand each other and work together, and many Western companies decide to expand their offshore operations. Cultural differences and the problems they lead to are real and should be addressed, but they are not the whole story, all appearances to the contrary. Our purpose in zeroing in on the cultural difficulties has not been to suggest that without solving these problems your offshore partnership is doomed, but only to say that if you do address these issues, your partnership will be even more successful—and successful that much sooner.

While we're looking on the bright side, we might also remind Western readers of the many qualities that make Indians such a pleasure to work with, why the same Indians who have you pulling your hair out in the afternoon are such a welcome sight the next morning. Among the many positive qualities Americans and Europeans regularly cite about Indians are these:

- Technical competence: Indians are very good at what they do.
- Strong work ethic: Indians are very hard-working, committed, and dedicated.
- Quick studies: Indians learn new things quickly.
- Desire to please: Indians want the client or the boss to be satisfied and will go to great lengths to make that happen.
- Respectful: Indians are extremely polite and deferential; they are very careful not to embarrass someone or hurt another person's feelings.
- Eager to learn: Younger Indians in particular get excited about learning new things, especially from the West.
- Loyal: Once Indians like and respect someone, they will do anything for that person.
- Easygoing: Indians tend not to be too serious or intense; they have a good sense of humor and always try to make the best of any situation.

If East-West partnerships work in spite of the cultural differences, which clearly they do, imagine how well they will work if the cultural differences are resolved.

How Long Does It Take?

Meanwhile, readers may be wondering what the timeline looks like for cultural adjustment; how soon they can expect to get beyond the most common misunderstandings and look forward to smooth sailing. The answer depends in part on the individuals involved in any particular East-West relationship; the more aware each one is of the culture of the other, the sooner they will identify cultural flashpoints and come up with a *modus operandi* for their relationship.

Naturally, Indians living in the West or with previous first-hand experience of the West are more likely to be aware of Western ways than Indians working remotely with Westerners. Americans and Europeans can expect the former to adjust more readily to Western norms and expectations, but they cannot expect Indians who have not had such exposure to be so quick to adapt. In this context, it's always a good idea when dealing with Indians to find out which ones have spent time in the West and which ones have not. For their part, Indians can expect Westerners with some first-hand experience of India to be more aware of their culture and know what to expect from Indians. As we have seen, though, the burden of adjustment usually falls more heavily on Indians.

Another factor in the adjustment timeline is the nature of a particular cultural difference that one side or the other is trying to get used to. The timeline for some adjustments can be quite short, a matter of days, while the timeline for others can be weeks or even months. Some cultural differences are superficial and minor; if a Westerner asks an Indian not to stand up every time he comes into the Indian's cubicle or not to use "sir" or "madam," most Indians can make this adjustment easily. But other cultural differences touch on deep-seated values and assumptions, and to change these behaviors can take some time. If you ask an Indian to be spontaneous and frank in giving negative feedback, he or she may initially find this very difficult, and you may have to give the individual a lot of encouragement and coaching. Still other cultural differences may be so deep that no amount of coaching or time is sufficient to get the

Indian to change the behavior. One example might be asking Indians to openly challenge or question something their superior says during a meeting.

Still another variable is the age of the Indian one is dealing with; for the most part, the younger the Indian, the more adaptable she is to Western ways. This is not only because young people in general tend to be more flexible and adaptable, but also because young Indians have not spent as much time in the Indian workplace as their elders and so may not be quite as "Indian" in their work habits.

Finally, in those Indian companies, or divisions of a company, that have been working longer with Western counterparts, there have no doubt been some cultural lessons learned along the way and passed on, in training or informally, to others. In these cases, the general level of cultural awareness will probably be higher than in companies that are just starting to work with the West. And the same will apply to Western companies.

If there is no single timeline for cultural adjustment, we can say that it is more likely to be a matter of months, rather than weeks, before colleagues from each side have a good grasp of where the other side is coming from and can regularly avoid most cultural misunderstandings. There will be incremental progress all along the way, of course, but the deep understanding that leads to changes in people's behavior and expectations does not come overnight. And we repeat again that whatever the timeline is for those working in each other's country, it is bound to be slower for those who stay in their home country and interact only by phone and e-mail.

In the meantime, Indians and Westerners might try to remember on occasion that along with all the misunderstanding and miscommunication inherent in working with foreigners, there is also the fascination of discovering a parallel universe where people think and act quite differently from you—and somehow manage to cope and even triumph. In discovering this universe, you also rediscover your own, seeing your behavior and your entire world from a new perspective.

Meanwhile, the skills you are learning—albeit the hard way, in some cases—are only going to be more in demand, not less, as time goes by. As business and work life become more and more globalized, the ability to work effectively with people from other cultures will increasingly distinguish those who will succeed in the workplace of the future from those who will be marginalized.

Bibliography

Adler, Nancy, 1986. *International Dimensions of Organizational Behavior.* Belmont, CA: Wadsworth, Inc.

Altbach, Philip. 2006. "Tiny At the Top." *Wilson Quarterly*, Autumn. 49–51.

Asselin, Gilles, and Ruth Mastron. 2001. *Au Contraire: Figuring Out the French.* Yarmouth, ME: Intercultural Press.

Bellman, Eric. 2006. "India's Cellphone Boom May Lose Charge." *The Wall Street Journal*, 23 August

Bijlani, Hiru. 1999. *Culture Shock: Succeed in Business India.* Singapore: Times Editions.

Bumiller, Elisabeth. 1990. *May You Be the Mother of A Hundred Sons: A Journey Among the Women of India.* New York: Fawcett Columbine.

"Can India Fly?" 2006. *The Economist*, 3 June, 13.

Carmel, Erran. 1999. *Global Software Teams: Collaborating Across Cultures and Time Zones.* Saddle River, NJ: Prentice Hall.

Carvajal, Doreen. 2006. "Dateline: India—The Long Arm of Offshoring Reaches into the News Industry." *International Herald Tribune*, 20 November, 12.

Coy, Peter. 2005. "Asian Competition: Is the Cup Half Empty—or Half Full?" *Business Week*, 22 August, 134–136.

Davies, Paul. 2004. *What's This India Business? Offshoring, Outsourcing, and the Global Services Revolution.* London: Nicholas Brealey International.

Devine, Elizabeth, and Nancy L. Braganti. 1986. *The Traveler's Guide to Asian Customs and Manners.* New York: St. Martin's Press.

Daniel, Diann. 2007, February 9. "How To Create A Good Relationship with Your Indian Vendor." *CIO Magazine*. Retrieved February 15, 2007, from http://www.cio.com/article/28703.

Dunung, Sanjyot. 1995. *Doing Business In Asia.* New York: Lexington Books.

Dwivedi, K.N. (ed). 2002. *Meeting the Needs of Ethnic Minority Children*. London: Jessica Kingsley.

Engardio, Pete. 2005. "A New World Economy." *Business Week*, 22 August, 52–58.

"Faster, Cheaper, Better." *The Economist*, 13 November 2004, 12–14.

Granered, Erik. 2005. *Global Call Centers: Achieving Outstanding Customer Service Across Cultures & Time Zones*. Boston, MA: Nicholas Brealey International.

Grimes, William. 2007. "The Power and the Potential of India's Economic Change." *The New York Times*, 17 January, E9.

Gudykunst, William B. and Stella Ting-Toomey. 1988. *Culture and Interpersonal Communication*. Newbury Park, CA: Sage.

Hamm, Steve. 2005. "Scrambling up the Development Ladder." *Business Week*, 22 August, 112–114.

Hamm, Steve. 2005. "Taking A Page From Toyota's Playbook." *Business Week*, 22 August, 69–72.

Henderson, Carl. 2002. *Culture and Customs of India*. Westport, CT: Greenwood Press.

Hickson, David J. ed. 1997. *Exploring Management Across the World*. London: Penguin Books.

Hickson, David J., and Derek S. Pugh. 1995. *Management Worldwide*. London: Penguin Books.

Hofstede, Geert. 1984. *Culture's Consequences: International Differences in Work-Related Values*, abridged ed. Beverly Hills, CA: Sage.

Huxley, Aldous. 1985. *Jesting Pilate*. London: Triad/Paladin.

"If in Doubt, Farm It Out." *The Economist*, 3 June 2006, 6–8.

"India Inc." *Time*, 26 June 2006, 38, 39.

Joshi, Manoj. 1997. *Passport India*. San Rafael, CA: World Trade Press.

Kamdar, Mira. 2007. *Planet India*. New York: Scribners.

Kammen, Michael. 1980. *People of Paradox*. Ithaca, NY: Cornell University Press.

Kanter, Rosabeth Moss. 1997. *On the Frontiers of Management*. Boston: Harvard Business School Press.

Kolanad, Gitanjali. 2005. *Culture Shock: India*. Singapore: Marshall Cavendish.

Kripalani, Manjeet. 2005. "Trying to Tame the Blackboard Jungle." *Business Week*, 22 August, 94–96.

Lannoy, Richard. 1971. *The Speaking Tree: A Study of Indian Culture and Society*. London: Oxford University Press.

Luce, Edward. 2007. *In Spite of the Gods: The Strange Rise of Modern India*. New York: Doubleday.

Manian, Ranjini. 2007. *Doing Business In India for Dummies*. New York: John Wiley and Sons.

McPhate, Mike. 2006. "Insults from America." *Long Island Newsday*, 11 January, A42.

Mehta, Pratap Bhanu quoted in Harrison, Lawrence 2006. *The Central Liberal Truth: How Politics Can Change A Culture and Save It from Itself*. Oxford: Oxford University Press, 117.

"Men and machines." *The Economist*, 13, June, 2004, 6–10.

Mishra, Pankaj. 2006. "The Myth of the New India." *The New York Times*, 6 July, A23.

Norris, Floyd. 2007. "Fearing Protectionism, In India." *The New York Times*, 26 January, C8.

"Now for the Hard Part." *The Economist*, 3 June 2006, 3,4.

Overby, Stephanie. 2007, February 1. "Secrets of Offshoring Success." *CIO Magazine*. Retrieved May 23, 2007, from http://www.cio.com/article/28492.

Prasad, Chandra, 2007. "Passage From India." *The New York Times Magazine*, 14 January, 74.

Rai, Saritha. 2005. "M.B.A. Students Bypassing Wall Street for a Summer in India." *The New York Times*, 5 August, C1.

Roberts, Sam. 2006. "Who Americans Are and What They Do in Census Data." *New York Times,* 15 December, 1.

Sen, Amartya. 2005. *The Argumentative Indian: Writings on Indian History, Culture, and Identity*. New York: Picador.

Sinha, Jai B.P. 1990. *Work Culture in the Indian Context*. New Delhi: Sage Publications.

Storti, Craig. 2001. *The Art of Crossing Cultures*. Yarmouth, ME: Intercultural Press.

———. 2004. *Americans At Work: A Guide to the Can-Do People*. Yarmouth, ME: Intercultural Press.

Tharoor, Shashi. 1997. *India: From Midnight to the Millenium and Beyond,* New York: Arcade Publishing.

Toppo, Greg. 2005. "Offshore Learning Online." *USA Today*, 30 August, D1, 2.

Virmani, B.P. 2007. *The Challenge of Indian Management*. New Delhi: Sage (Response Books).

"Virtual champions." *The Economist*, 3 June 2006, 4–6.

Wolpert, Stanley. 2005. *India*. Berkeley, CA: University of California.

"World of Work." *The Economist*, 13 November 2004, 3, 4.

About the Author

Craig Storti specializes in the design and delivery of seminars in intercultural communications and global business dynamics for clients from government, business, and the education sectors, including:

- Euronext
- British Telecom
- FedEx
- Chase
- Pfizer
- Best Buy

- Ernst & Young
- ExxonMobil
- NIKE
- Target
- Federal Aviation Administration

- The United Nations
- U.S. Department of State
- NASA
- FBI

Since 1995 Mr. Storti has been conducting seminars in Indian-Western cultural differences for numerous U.S. and European customers (financial institutions, insurance companies, major retailers) and their Indian offshore service providers (TCS, Cognizant, Wipro, Infosys) to help these companies minimize the impact of cultural differences on IT and BPO collaborations and other offshore ventures.

Mr. Storti is the author of six previous books, several of which have become standards in the field, including:

- *The Art of Crossing Cultures*
- *The Art of Coming Home*
- *Cross-Cultural Dialogues*
- *Figuring Foreigners Out*

- *Old World/New World: Americans and Europeans*
- *Americans At Work: A Cultural Guide to the Can-Do People*

A well-known presenter, Mr. Storti is represented by the European Speakers Bureau and the Washington Speakers Bureau and has written for a number of national magazines and major newspapers, including *The Washington Post*, *The Los Angeles Times*, and the *Chicago Tribune*. He has lived nearly a quarter of his life abroad—with extended stays in Moslem, Hindu, and Buddhist cultures—and speaks French and Arabic.

Web site: craigstorti.com
E-mail: craig@craigstorti.com

Index